# Transitions

Phil Clark started his career in the early 1970s as an actor in Theatre in Education (TIE) and Community Theatre. In the 1980s he was director of TIE and Community Theatre at the Crucible Theatre, Sheffield. Throughout the 1990s he was Artistic Director of the Sherman Theatre in Cardiff. He now works throughout Britain as a freelance theatre director and writer.

# Transitions

**Edited by Phil Clark**

Parthian
The Old Surgery
Napier Street
Cardigan
SA43 1ED

www.parthianbooks.co.uk

First published in 2008
© The authors/the theatre companies 2005
This collection © Parthian 2008
All Rights Reserved

ISBN 978-1-902638-47-8

Cover design by Lucy Llewellyn
Inner design & typsetting by books@lloydrobson.com
Printed and bound by Dinefwr Press, Llandybïe, Wales

Published with the financial support of the Welsh
Books Council

British Library Cataloguing in Publication Data – A
cataloguing record for this book is available from the
British Library

# Contents

# Introduction

When I arrived in 1990 to take up the post of Artistic Director of the Sherman Theatre, Cardiff – the only producing theatre in the capital city – I quickly realised that my prior eighteen years experience of professional theatre in England bore very little relationship to the theatre activity in Wales.

For the previous seven years I had been a director at the Crucible Theatre in Sheffield. Within an hour's travel I could have seen professional repertory theatre in Leeds, York, Manchester, Oldham, Bolton, Nottingham, Derby, and Chesterfield, alongside numerous Young People's Theatre (YPT), Theatre in Education (TIE), and small-scale theatre companies. Having arrived in Cardiff, my nearest repertory theatre was Bristol Old Vic, ironically, in England. To see the work of the other producing theatres in Wales meant travelling some three to four hours, to Mold in Flintshire; Bangor in Gwynedd; or Milford Haven in Pembrokeshire. There were, however, numerous YPT, TIE, and small-scale theatre companies in Cardiff, and within a fifty-mile radius.

It was immediately clear to me that the produced theatre of Wales was going to be vastly different from that I had known in England, firstly because there was so little of it; secondly because it was so geographically spread out, and therefore it was difficult to maintain a professional dialogue; and thirdly because the majority of work for writers, directors, designers, and actors was not on big stages in Wales, but predominantly within the YPT, TIE and small-scale touring theatre movement.

Theatre writing in the English language in Wales continues to be in its infancy. It is only in the second half of the twentieth century that we can begin to chart any substantial growth in professional, English-language theatre. Wales has always had an extremely productive and imaginative amateur drama movement, in both the English and Welsh languages. With the emergence of television and radio in the 1950s, Wales began to see the development of playwrights such as Dylan Thomas, T C Thomas, Dannie Abse, and Gwyn Thomas, and as the century progressed new writers emerged, including Peter Gill, Frank Vickery, Alan Osborne, Charles Way, Ian Rowlands, Edward Thomas, and more recently Tim Rhys, Helen Griffin, Lisa Hunt, and Gary Owen, to name but a few.

It was clear to me on my arrival that all Wales-based theatre artists had to diversify in order to make a living. They had to be able to work on stage, in film and television, as well as radio. Of course the artists in England had to do the same, but one of my first observations was how much more competitive the market was in Wales, predominantly because there was less work being commissioned and created, and because there was a large and growing artistic community that predominantly wanted to work on their home turf.

Although there were many negative factors within this situation, there were also positive conclusions. This book sets out to record some of these conclusions, as a result of the artists having to diversify and re-invent themselves in various artistic and theatrical forms. I have therefore included in this volume work by established writers and theatre companies, with some of them working in a medium for the first time, and some of them creating work that had to exist in two mediums simultaneously, ie. stage and television. What we begin to observe are predominantly writers and other artists working in transition in order to survive, professionally and artistically.

*The Watching* – a play for young people – was devised, written, and performed by Gwent Theatre in Abergavenny. It tells the true story of a young girl in West Wales who starved herself, and the effect of her actions, both locally and nationally. It is a very moving story which asks big, emotional questions of its audience.

Gwent Theatre is one of Wales' longest running YPT and TIE Companies. They run a highly successful youth theatre and also perform shows for adults in their immediate community. There is a genuine dialogue between Gwent Theatre and the schools in the area. Consequently, when they present cutting edge and often difficult shows in schools, such as *The Watching*, teachers and students find it an enriching and valuable educational experience. Gwent Theatre is a prime example of success in Wales, and proof that a long-term funding strategy ensures a positive and fruitful dialogue between a theatre company and its audience. This work also demonstrates how well-crafted theatre can be created through a devising process, one that is usual within the YPT and TIE movement throughout Britain.

*Wishful Thinking* was devised by Cardiff-based Hijinx Theatre. They create theatre for community audiences throughout Britain. Over the years they have specialized in creating plays for people with learning difficulties. *Wishful Thinking* explores the emotional needs of three women within one family. It is a highly-charged piece of theatre that is written and targeted at a specific audience in a specific environment, ie. day care centres. This is indeed 'special' work and demands of its creators and performers specialist knowledge. It's important that this work receives the same status as any other theatre in the country. There is every possibility that the general public will never experience this beautiful work, and that is why it is important to include it in this anthology.

Hijinx continue to develop high-quality theatre for audiences with special needs and/or learning difficulties. Their work is an important contribution to the canon of English-language theatre in Wales.

Gillian Clarke is one of Wales' celebrated living poets. Her first play for radio, *Talking to Wordsworth*, was commissioned by BBC Radio Wales' drama department and the Sherman Theatre, as part of their six-year partnership – a partnership that produced thirty new plays broadcast live from the Sherman Theatre Studio, in front of a live audience. Again, this season introduced many new playwrights to Welsh audiences and was particularly successful in commissioning many new emerging writers.

*Talking to Wordsworth* is set in the occupational therapy department of a mental hospital. As the visiting poet introduces the patients to the joys of poetry and the spoken word, she also releases one of the patients from years of mental solitude, as he recites Wordsworth's poem 'Daffodils' out loud. The audience – in both the hospital and the theatre – are included, as if he was 'talking to Wordsworth'. Gillian's beautiful, poetic play is based on her own experiences as a visiting poet in schools, hospitals, and day care centres.

Charles Way is one of Wales' most prolific playwrights. He writes mainly for the stage and has specialized in work for young audiences. Charles was Writer in Residence for twelve months at the Sherman Theatre and BBC Radio Wales, as a result of the partnership and added support from the Arts Council of Wales. His extended dramatic poem, *The Gate*, was written during this residency, and broadcast by BBC Radio Wales. It is a play for voices that explores the relationship between father and son. The 'gate' is a metaphor for all the decisions we make in life – some painful, others joyous, but all necessary.

In the mid-1990s the Sherman Theatre had a unique partnership with HTV Wales. Over a five year period, they jointly commissioned Welsh and Wales-based writers to write new plays that could be performed on stage at the Sherman Theatre as part of their Lunchtime Theatre Season, and then televised and screened by HTV Wales. This was a terrific partnership that produced over twenty new plays for Wales. Many of them continue to be performed all over the world. One of those commissions was *Break My Heart* by Arnold Wesker.

Arnold lives in Hay-on-Wye and is one of Britain's leading and most influential playwrights. *Break My Heart* is a beautiful and painful play that examines the relationship between a husband and his wife in the South Wales valleys, as she strives to better herself by studying the works of Shakespeare. Threatened by his wife's newfound knowledge and use of language, the husband resorts to physical and verbal abuse of his wife. The marriage is breaking down. The wife's heart is broken, but knowledge has empowered her. The play dares to venture into the often unspoken realms of society. It is timeless, and masterfully written.

So these are not ordinary plays. Often they are specific in both form and content. They are the result of artists taking risks, or trying something new in their professional lives. I think these plays reflect the peculiarity of Welsh theatre, and because we are a small and diverse nation, it is right that our theatre should reflect this diversity.

If we are to see a development in English-language theatre in Wales, then the future should be about partnership between stage, television, film, and radio, and these plays prove that the artists of Wales are able to work across the live and recorded medias. What Wales needs is a culture of partnership and collaboration that empowers its artists and places the audience at the centre of the dramatic experience, as is demonstrated by the plays in this eclectic collection.

Phil Clark

# The Watching

**Gwent Theatre**

First performed at Cross Keys College
1 October 1991.

Cast:

| | | |
|---|---|---|
| Sarah Jacob | – | Erica Eirian |
| Evan Jacob<br>Dr Henry Davies | – | Michael Foulkes |
| Hannah Jacob | – | Nicky Thompson |
| Margaret<br>Sister Clinch | – | Carys Llewelyn |
| Rev Evan Jones | – | Gary Meredith |

Creative Team:

| | | |
|---|---|---|
| Artistic Director | – | Gary Meredith |
| Designer | – | Bettina Reeves |
| Incidental Music | – | Tim Riley |
| Stage Manager | – | Debbie Rees |
| Set Construction | – | John Noble |
| Costumes | – | Yvonne Owens |
| Teachers' Pack | – | Jayne Davies |
| Administrative Director | – | Julia Davies |
| Secretary | – | Christine Miller |

Devised and written by the cast, for 5th and 6th form pupils and college students. Special thanks to John Lovat for assistance during preparation, devising, and rehearsals. Thanks to David Freeman, Tredegar House; Walter Jones, Welsh Folk Museum; Gallup and Rivers; Gareth Roberts.

# ACT ONE
## The Unstoppable Chain of Events
## The World of Sarah Jacob

*The action takes place between 1867 and 1869.*

SARAH: Sarah Jacob.

CHORUS: Nine years old...

CHORUS: Bright...

CHORUS: Pretty...

CHORUS: Determined...

CHORUS: A liking for religion...

CHORUS: And for reading...

CHORUS: Father:

EVAN: Evan.

CHORUS: Mother:

HANNAH: Hannah.

CHORUS: Three brothers...

CHORUS: Three sisters...

CHORUS: Her favourite:

MARGARET: Margaret. (*Calling*) Sarah, Sarah. Play with me, Sarah.

SARAH: What do you want to play, Margaret?

MARGARET: (*Singing*) Ji geffyl bach yn cario ni'n dau...

SARAH: (*Singing*) Ji geffyl bach yn cario ni'n dau...

MARGARET/SARAH: (*Singing*)
>Dros y ynydd I hela cnau
>Dwr yn yr afon a'r cerrig yn slip
>Gwympon ni'n dau – wel dyna chi dric!
>(*They laugh.*)

CHORUS: The Jacobs live on a small farm...

CHORUS: Lletherneuadd-Uchaf...

CHORUS: In the parish of Llanfihangel Ar Arth...

CHORUS: In the beautiful Teifi Valley...

CHORUS: Up the winding hillside...

CHORUS: High on the moorland...

CHORUS: Some one hundred and twenty acres...

CHORUS: Rent sixty-one pound per year...

GOSSIP: Never any difficulty collecting their money...

GOSSIP: As respectable a family as ever went to the Congregational Chapel in Pencader.

EVAN: Come on Sarah, wake up, it's dawn – time for milking.

HANNAH: Sarah, it's your turn to rock the baby.

EVAN: Help your brother pick the potatoes, Sarah.

HANNAH: Go and collect the eggs for me, Sarah.

EVAN: Sarah, come here, look...

*SARAH hesitates.*

EVAN: A new calf.

*SARAH looks, nervously.*

EVAN: No need to be afraid. Look, a new calf, a new born calf, a new born miracle.

SARAH: (*Smiling*) A miracle.

REV JONES: (*Singing*)
    All things bright and beautiful
    All creatures great and small...

EVERYONE: (*Singing*)
    All things wise and wonderful
    The Lord God made them all.

REV JONES: Not only are you the prettiest little girl in Sunday school, Sarah, but you are also the cleverest.

*He gives SARAH a Bible.*

SARAH: Thank you, Vicar. (*Calling*) Mam, Dad, I've won a Bible, I've won a Bible – for reading!

EVAN: Well done, Sarah.

HANNAH: Good girl, Sarah.

EVAN: You always were the clever one. We're very proud of you, aren't we, Hannah? And as you've been such a good girl we've got something for you too.

HANNAH: (*Holding out her hands*) Which hand?

*SARAH points – revealing the present.*

EVAN: For your hair.

HANNAH: Your favourite colour.

SARAH: (*Calling*) Margaret, Margaret, look at my ribbon.

MARGARET: Can I have one, Mam?

EVAN: When you do as well as Sarah.

HANNAH: We'll see.

MARGARET: I'm gonna have one, Sarah.

SARAH: Can I read to you from my Bible, Dada?

HANNAH: Not now Sarah – Dada hasn't had his supper yet.

MARGARET: You can read to me, Sarah – teach me to read.

SARAH: I want to read to Dada.

MARGARET: Read to me, Sarah.

SARAH: I want to read to Dada. Mam?

HANNAH: Read to Margaret, Sarah.

EVAN: (*Tenderly*) Hannah, Hannah, let Sarah read to us. We'll all listen to Sarah read.

SARAH: (*Reading from her Bible*)
    The Lord is my shepherd I shall not want
    He maketh me to lie down in green pastures
    He leadeth me beside the still waters
    He restoreth my soul:
    He guideth me in the paths of righteousness
    for his name's sake...

*EVAN joins in.*

    Yea, though I walk through the valley of
    the shadow of death, I will fear no evil;
    for thou art with me: thy rod and thy staff,
    they comfort me...

CHILDREN: (*Chanting*)
    Sarah Jacob's the teacher's pet
    Sarah Jacob's the teacher's pet
    Sarah Jacob's the teacher's pet
    Teacher's pet...
    Teacher's pet...
    Teacher's pet...

SARAH: Just because I'm clever.

CHILDREN: (*Chanting*)
> Sarah's a clever clogs
> Sarah's a clever clogs
> Sarah's a clever clogs...

SARAH: Just because I'm bright.

CHILD: My mam says you're just like your dad. You think you're better than us.

SARAH: I don't.

CHILD: My mam says you've got airs and graces.

SARAH: I haven't.

CHILD: My mam says you're a right little madam.

SARAH: I'm not.

CHILD: What you gonna be when you grow up, Sarah Jacob?

SARAH: Different.

CHILD: Sarah, my sister's gone to work in the big house – no more dirty farmwork for her.

SARAH: When I grow up I'm going to live in the big house, not work in it.

CHILD: My dad says that your dad works your mam's fingers to the bone and if he's not careful she'll end up in an early grave.

CHILD: My little sister's gone to an early grave, Sarah, but my mam says it's alright because she's gone to heaven.

CHILD: Do you believe in heaven, Sarah?

SARAH: Of course I do.

CHILD: And hell?

CHILD: (*Whispering*) Psst. Psst. Everyone. Everyone. Psst. Sarah! Let's go and scrump apples in Reverend Jones' orchard.

CHILDREN: Yeah!

CHILD: Big, red, juicy apples!

CHILDREN: Yeah!

CHILD: Sarah. Sarah?

CHILDREN: Sarah. Sarah?

SARAH: I'll keep watch.

REV JONES: Sarah? Sarah, what are you doing here?

SARAH: Just watching, Vicar. Just watching.

CHILDREN: (*Chanting*)
> Sarah's a tell-tale
> Sarah's a tell-tale
> Sarah's a tell-tale
> Sarah's a tell-tale

Tell tale, tell-tale
Tell tale, tell-tale....

*SARAH retreats to her bed. HANNAH removes SARAH's dress and helps her into bed.*

## The Onset of Illness

HANNAH: Good girl, Sarah. Say your prayers now like a good girl.

SARAH: (*Crying*) I've got a pain, Mam, I've got a pain. It hurts. It hurts.

HANNAH: Where, Sarah?

SARAH: (*Still crying and pointing to her stomach*) Here, here, it hurts, Mam, it hurts bad. Make it go away. Make it go away.

HANNAH: (*Rubbing SARAH'S stomach*) Alright, Sarah, alright. Ssh. Ssh.

EVAN: What's that on her pillow?

HANNAH: (*Looking*) Blood.

EVAN: She's been coughing up blood?

CHORUS: The doctor is summoned...

CHORUS: He applies remedies to relieve the pain...

CHORUS: But no sooner is the pain controlled...

*SARAH has a fit – a strong convulsive fit.*

DOCTOR ONE: Inflammation of the pleura!

CHORUS: The fits continue...

CHORUS: Sarah loses weight...

CHORUS: She's reduced almost to a skeleton...

DOCTOR TWO: Give her rice, milk and oatmeal gruel.

CHORUS: For a whole month Sarah lies in a kind of permanent fit...

CHORUS: Barely conscious...

CHORUS: Lying on her back...

CHORUS: Her muscles rigid...

DOCTOR TWO: I really am unable to identify her complaint or to suggest any remedy to relieve her.

CHORUS: Others are consulted...

DOCTOR ONE: In my opinion she has an incurable inflammation of the brain.

DOCTOR TWO: Had I been called earlier I may have been able to help.

DOCTOR ONE: Here, try these...

HANNAH: But she can't swallow, Doctor. She's taken nothing for a month. A whole month. All I've been able to give her is a little water and table beer to moisten her lips.

DOCTOR TWO: Has she passed water?

HANNAH: A little.

DOCTOR ONE: Have her bowels been relieved?

HANNAH: In very small quantities.

DOCTOR TWO: (*Examining SARAH*) She's almost pulseless. The upper part of her belly is retracted, however the lower part full and hard. We can hope for some change in the next two or three days.

CHORUS: Friday – Saturday – Sunday...

SARAH: (*Calling*) Mam, Mam, can I have a drink of milk?

DOCTOR ONE: Now remember: milk, rice and oatmeal gruel, that will soon have her back on her feet.

CHORUS: But Sarah remains in bed...

CHORUS: Throughout March...

CHORUS: April...

SARAH: May the twelfth.

HANNAH: Happy birthday, Sarah.

EVAN: Happy birthday, Sarah.

CHORUS: Happy birthday, Sarah.

CHORUS: Sarah Jacob.

HANNAH: Ten years old.

CHORUS: Sarah's losing her hair...

CHORUS: Every so often she loses consciousness...

CHORUS: Brought on by a dog barking...

CHORUS: Or sometimes by being touched...

CHORUS: Or by the sight...

CHORUS: Or mere mention...

CHORUS: Of food.

## Scene One

*HANNAH washes SARAH's face.*

HANNAH: There we are. (*She goes to leave.*)

SARAH: Mam. Will you do my hair?

HANNAH: In a while, Sarah, just let me see to the baby.

SARAH: (*Coughs*) I've got a pain.

*SARAH coughs and shows the blood on her hand to HANNAH who returns to the bed and wipes the blood away.*

13

HANNAH: D'you feel better after that little wash?

SARAH: Mmm.

*HANNAH starts to do SARAH's hair.*

SARAH: Can I have my ribbons?

HANNAH: In a while, let me just do your hair.

SARAH: I've got a pain, Mam, it hurts – it's bad.

*HANNAH picks up a piece of lace and puts it around SARAH's shoulders.*

HANNAH: This is the piece of lace I wore the day I married Dada.

SARAH: It's pretty, I like it. Do I look pretty?

HANNAH: You look pretty as a flower.

SARAH: What kind of a flower?

HANNAH: What kind of flower would you like to look like?

SARAH: A sweet pea. (*Laughing*) A sweet pea.

*SARAH coughs more blood into her hand. HANNAH wipes it away.*

SARAH: Mami, Mami, Mami.

HANNAH: Come on, be brave my little sweet pea.

SARAH: Sweet pea, sweet pea, I'm a sweet pea...

*EVAN enters.*

SARAH: Look, Dada! (*She holds up the lace.*)

*EVAN smiles, looks at HANNAH then back to SARAH.*

SARAH: I've got a pain. Make it go away.

EVAN: Would you like some milk?

SARAH: No, no. It'll make it worse; it'll make my pain worse. Make it go away.

EVAN: Have you eaten anything today?

*SARAH doesn't reply.*

EVAN: (*To HANNAH*) For goodness sake woman, what kind of mother are you? The child must eat if she's to get better. You're here in the house with her all day. I'm out in the fields. You're her mother, it's your duty to make her eat. You're failing in your duty, you are failing as a mother, you are failing...

SARAH: Dada! Please, please be nice to Mami.

EVAN: It's alright, Sarah, it's alright. Hisht, hisht.

SARAH: Promise me you'll be nice to Mam. Promise me. Promise me. Promise me.

EVAN: I promise. Hannah!

*HANNAH fetches milk.*

SARAH: (*Seeing it*) No. Noo!

EVAN: Come on Sarah, you must try. There's a good girl, just a spoonful. (*To HANNAH*) Give it to her.

*HANNAH attempts to force-feed SARAH with the milk.*

SARAH: It hurts. It hurts.

EVAN: Milk is good for you, come on, there's a good girl. Give it to her – make her swallow it.

SARAH: No. Please. It hurts.

EVAN: Swallow it. Make her swallow it. Just one mouthful. Give it to her.

SARAH: No. No.

EVAN: Make her drink it. Make her.

SARAH: No. No. It hurts. You're hurting me. Why are you doing this to me?

*HANNAH leaves EVAN and SARAH to it. SARAH has a full-scale fit.*

EVAN: Alright. Alright. Lie down. It's alright, put your head on the pillow.

SARAH: You don't love me.

EVAN: We're worried about you. We do love you.

SARAH: Then promise me you'll never do that again. Promise me you'll never bring food or drink into this room again.

EVAN: Sarah!

SARAH: (*Offering her Bible*) Swear!

*EVAN puts his hand on the Bible.*

GOSSIP (*The actor who plays Rev Jones*): Sarah Jacob's been in bed for eight months now. Poor thing.

SARAH: Margaret!

*MARGARET sits on the bed.*

GOSSIP: She hasn't eaten anything for nearly a month they say. Can't bear the sight of food. Or water. It's unnatural.

*IMAGE: MARGARET and SARAH laughing.*

EVAN: What do they find to laugh about?

HANNAH: Something and nothing.

EVAN: Whatever, it's good to hear laughter in the house, good to see them happy – Sarah so happy.

HANNAH: It's been four weeks now, Evan.

EVAN: But she's looking better, Hannah, so much better.

HANNAH: I know.

17

EVAN: The Almighty is watching over her.

HANNAH: But she's restless – at night. I can hear her – tossing and turning, calling out.

EVAN: Calling out what?

HANNAH: I don't know.

EVAN: Don't worry, Hannah.

HANNAH: I suppose the best thing to do is to carry on as normal – not make her feel too different.

*During the following gossip sequence, MARGARET dresses SARAH with a bridal head-dress adorned with ribbons.*

GOSSIP: It's not normal...

GOSSIP: If she hears a dog bark she has a fit...

GOSSIP: If she's touched she has a fit...

GOSSIP: If you ask me she is touched...

GOSSIP: The parents can't take food into her room...

GOSSIP: She's not sleeping well, they say...

GOSSIP: Talks about heaven and hell all the time...

GOSSIP: I thought they said she was looking better?

GOSSIP: Well, she is...

GOSSIP: Mind, they've called the vicar.

## Scene Two

REV JONES: Mrs Jacob, there's a lot of talk in the village – rumours, idle gossip. It's being said that Sarah hasn't had anything to eat for almost a month now.

HANNAH: That's true, Vicar. But that's not the reason I sent word for you to call.

REV JONES: Oh, I see.

*Pause.*

HANNAH: No, it's her dreams – she's having strange dreams, visions you might say, all about hell and damnation. She's troubled by them. She's full of questions and she's not happy with the answers we give her, so we sent for you. She asked us to.

REV JONES: I'm glad you sent for me.

HANNAH: (*Calling*) Sarah, the Reverend Jones is here to see you. Margaret, come here.

REV JONES: Margaret. Hello Sarah. How are you? I fancy you look a little paler since the last time I saw you.

SARAH: I'm quite well, Vicar, although I do feel a little weak today. You haven't been to see me.

REV JONES: I've been very busy, Sarah. There are lots of people I have to...

SARAH: You said I was the cleverest and prettiest girl in Sunday school.

REV JONES: I did, Sarah, yes I did. Your mother tells me...

SARAH: I could have died. I coughed blood – red blood all over the white sheets. Why didn't you come – before? To see me? Do you know I don't eat? I used to, but I don't now – it gave me a pain, I used to eat little bits, but it hurt so now I don't eat at all. It's God's will. God's will that I don't eat.

REV JONES: Why do you think this is, Sarah?

SARAH: Because I feel better when I don't eat and I say my prayers and read my Bible. I think this is God's will but I'm not sure. Do you think that God...

REV JONES: God is watching over all of us, Sarah. He knows our thoughts, secrets – we can't hide anything from God.

SARAH: Do you think I'll go to heaven? You think I'm good, don't you?

REV JONES: Yes, I believe you are, but if you do have any secrets, Sarah...

SARAH: I can't sleep sometimes.

REV JONES: Wouldn't it be better if you tried to eat something?

SARAH: I don't need to eat.

REV JONES: But now that the illness has passed...

SARAH: I don't want to talk about it. (*Pause.*) Tell me about heaven.

REV JONES: If we try to lead good lives...

SARAH: And I'm good, aren't I, Vicar?

REV JONES: Yes.

SARAH: What if we die with sin in our souls?

REV JONES: If we have been truly bad, Sarah, and we have not sought forgiveness, then we will surely go to hell.

SARAH: Do you believe that if you sin and say you're sorry you can still go to heaven?

REV JONES: Yes, if you are truly sorry, the Lord Jesus Christ will forgive you. But if you have offended God in any way, Sarah, you can tell me and we can pray together if you like. (*Pause.*) Do you fear you might go to hell, Sarah?

SARAH: I do wish you came to see me more often, Vicar. You see I'm so weak I can't come to you, but I think if I joined your church properly you could watch over me like God watches over me. It would be such a comfort – it's such a burden.

REV JONES: Why?

SARAH: It just feels like a burden. God has chosen to watch over me in this particular way.

REV JONES: Sarah, do you understand what is meant by vanity?

SARAH: Vanity? That's when you care too much about how you look, isn't it?

REV JONES: It can be. But it can also be thinking we are more important than we are. Like Lucifer.

SARAH: The Devil!

REV JONES: He thought he was more important, better than God Himself – and the brightest of angels became the Guardian of Hell.

SARAH: Lucifer didn't say he was sorry, did he?

REV JONES: No.

SARAH: If he had, he might have been made an angel again.

REV JONES: If he'd been truly sorry.

SARAH: I wish I could sleep. When I'm awake I worry. Sometimes I'm awake all night and I don't know sometimes whether I'm dreaming or not. Sometimes I don't read my poetry book. Do you know why? It's to show God, to show Him I can do without things, to prove to Him I'm pure of heart. Do you think I'm remarkable – because I don't eat?

REV JONES: Yes – very.

SARAH: It must be because I pray – and God is watching over me.

REV JONES: Sarah, you should be outside – in the sunshine, playing with Margaret, the other children...

SARAH: Did I tell you about my foot?

REV JONES: No.

SARAH: Sometimes I can't move it. Do you like my ribbons?

REV JONES: I do.

SARAH: You said I was the cleverest and the prettiest little girl in Sunday school. Did you pray for me?

REV JONES: I did.

SARAH: This is Mam's wedding veil – it doesn't matter, does it?

REV JONES: It looks nice.

SARAH: Can I join your church properly so that we can have more chats like this?

REV JONES: Of course you can.

SARAH: At night, when it's dark, I can't sleep, and I worry, (*she reaches out and touches his hand*) but you're such a comfort to me. I'm getting better, aren't I? God is showing me that I can get better without food or drink. He's telling me, isn't he?

REV JONES: (*Withdrawing his hand*) Try to sleep and not to worry. (*He leaves.*)

GOSSIP: Well I think it's a sign...

GOSSIP: I've seen her...

GOSSIP: She made my boy better...

GOSSIP: I think it's unnatural...

GOSSIP: She touched my boy and the fever left him...

GOSSIP: If you don't eat or drink you die...

GOSSIP: She's been blessed by God...

GOSSIP: I feel sorry for the other children...

GOSSIP: I feel sorry for the mother...

GOSSIP: Reverend Jones has been going there a lot...

GOSSIP: There's people in and out all the time...

GOSSIP: She must be eating...

GOSSIP: Or at least drinking...

GOSSIP: You die otherwise...

GOSSIP: God works in mysterious ways...

GOSSIP: The mother says it's a miracle...

GOSSIP: Well, why not? Greater wonders have happened before...

GOSSIP: I don't believe it...

GOSSIP: I'm glad she's not my daughter...

GOSSIP: Miracles happen to those who believe in them.

## Scene Three

REV JONES: I have prayed to the Almighty for enlightenment as to what is happening in this house. I believe that you are honest people and that Sarah is a special child. But she is not a miracle. It is inconceivable that she could have gone without food or drink for so long. I think she's confused, she is deluding herself.

EVAN: When Sarah was very ill, I forced her to eat, it caused her great pain. She made me swear a solemn oath that I would never do that again, or bring food into her presence. And since that day the child has blossomed, bloomed. Hannah?

HANNAH: It's true, Vicar. Since that day not a morsel of food has passed her lips.

EVAN: Y Doctor Mawr, the hand of God has touched her, it is a miracle.

REV JONES: Evan, I do not doubt the sincerity of your faith for one moment, but you are a farmer and you know yourself a lamb that does not suckle dies. (*He quotes from his Bible – Isaiah*) 'He shall feed his flock like a shepherd, he shall gather the lambs in his arm and carry them in his bosom, and shall gently lead those that give suck.'

25

EVAN: Our Lord Jesus fasted for forty days and forty nights and was tempted by the Devil, and He did not die because it was the will of God. Have faith, Vicar.

HANNAH: You are an educated man, Vicar – we are simple farm people, but we know what we know. Sarah is blessed. This is a miracle.

EVAN: We believe. Why can't you?

SARAH: (*Calling*) Reverend Jones. Reverend Jones.

*With a look towards EVAN and HANNAH, REV JONES goes to SARAH.*

SARAH: Look Vicar, look. Look out of the window. It's a beautiful day. The blue sky, the green fields. Sometimes I wish I could be out there.

REV JONES: You could be, Sarah.

SARAH: No, Vicar. If God wanted me to be out there He would not confine me to my bed.

REV JONES: It is not natural, Sarah, for a young healthy girl to confine herself to her bed in this way.

SARAH: It is God's will, Vicar, not mine. (*Pause.*) Do you believe in God's will, in prayer, in abstinence? Many people abstain for the good of their souls, for the good of others. Sometimes we have to do things even though we'd rather be doing something else. I expect there are times when you'd rather be fishing than writing your sermons?

REV JONES: (*Laughing*) Sarah, there are times when I am fishing when I can be thinking about what it is I want to say in my sermons.

SARAH: Do you believe you'll go to heaven, Vicar?

REV JONES: I hope so.

SARAH: Do you believe your wife is in heaven?

REV JONES: Indeed I hope so. She was a good Christian woman, she led a good Christian life.

SARAH: If she was so good, why did God let her suffer?

REV JONES: God doesn't intervene directly in everyone's life in that sort of way. Some things are meant to be.

SARAH: Did you pray to God for her suffering to stop?

REV JONES: I did. And she was relieved of her pain in death. I comfort myself that she is in heaven and that one day we will be reunited there.

SARAH: So you do believe in heaven?

REV JONES: Sarah, you know I do.

SARAH: And hell?

REV JONES: Yes.

SARAH: And life after death?

REV JONES: Yes.

SARAH: And in God's will?

REV JONES: Yes.

SARAH: And yet you seek and expect no proof of these things.

REV JONES: Why all these questions, Sarah?

SARAH: Faith, Reverend Jones. Isn't that what faith is? Faith is a gift from God and only He knows who has it. (*Pause.*) Shall we read together?

REV JONES: If you would like to, Sarah.

SARAH: (*Takes her Bible and reads*) 'Then was Jesus led up of the spirit into the wilderness to be tempted of the Devil. And when He had fasted forty days and forty nights He afterward hungered. And the tempter came and said unto Him, if thou art the Son of God, command...'

REV JONES: 'That these stones become bread. But he answered and said, It is written man shall not live by bread alone, but by every word that proceedeth out of the mouth of God.'

*REV JONES looks directly at SARAH. She smiles and closes her eyes. This is the moment where REV JONES begins to believe that SARAH really is a miracle. He reaches out and touches her gently on her forehead. As he does so, SARAH's gloved right hand appears from beneath the bedclothes and gently takes his hand away. She opens her eyes, smiles at him, and then closes her eyes as if in sleep.*

GOSSIP: The father says she's being watched over by Y Doctor Mawr...

GOSSIP: He's a stubborn man...

GOSSIP: Once his mind's made up about something there's no turning him back...

GOSSIP: They're a respectable family...

GOSSIP: Very religious people...

GOSSIP: Well, he is at any rate...

GOSSIP: Ignorant, you mean...

GOSSIP: You're just jealous because she's not your daughter...

GOSSIP: I've seen her – she looks like an angel...

GOSSIP: I believe...

GOSSIP: You'd believe anything...

GOSSIP: My husband won't let me near the place...

GOSSIP: I only know if you don't eat or drink you die...

GOSSIP: Well, she's not dead...

GOSSIP: You can't deny that the family are good, honest people...

GOSSIP: People will believe what they want to believe...

GOSSIP: She's always been a very devout child...

GOSSIP: Close to God.

REV JONES: Miracles happen to those who believe in them.

## Scene Four

REV JONES: My dear Henry, there are no doubts left in my mind – not a shadow of a doubt remains. Sarah Jacob is a miracle!

DR DAVIES: Please, Evan – sit down!

REV JONES: I would rather stand.

DR DAVIES: Evan!

REV JONES: I have come here to give you my opinion on this matter and all you can do is sit there with that insufferable grin on your face!

DR DAVIES: Please – sit down Evan.

REV JONES: I will not, sir. I prefer to stand, thank you.

DR DAVIES: Very well. As you please. But you must forgive my scepticism. I am a doctor, Evan, a man of science – and a man of science cannot allow himself to permit the possibility...

REV JONES: Exactly – you are blinded by your profession, you will not see further than your nose-end, but I would remind you, sir, that there are more things in heaven and earth than mankind will ever have the capacity to understand.

DR DAVIES: Evan, I can see this girl means a lot to you and she is, by all accounts, an extraordinary creature.

REV JONES: She is! Remarkable. Truly a child of God. Serene, calm, asking the most profound questions. Do you know, for the first time since my dear wife died, I feel I can see clearly. I woke up this morning and I laughed, just laughed for no other reason than the sheer joy of being alive. I feel as though I have been reborn.

DR DAVIES: Evan, you are my oldest and my dearest friend and it is plain to me that you are transformed, elated, and I am pleased to see you in such a happy frame of mind. However, as a friend I must tell you that people are laughing. They say that the father is mad, or worse, and if you start going around proclaiming miracles they'll say the same about you. And I do not wish to see you make a fool of yourself, Evan.

REV JONES: I am not mad. I have seen the child, spoken to her, to her parents – many times now, and I am convinced they are telling the truth. I have prayed, I have examined my conscience time after time. And in the end it was all so simple. I refused to believe the evidence of my eyes. But when I stopped denying the truth of what God had placed before me, a weight was lifted from my shoulders. God himself has restored my faith through the miracle of Sarah Jacob. Henry, do not judge me, go and see the child for yourself – examine her and you will confirm the truth of my words.

DR DAVIES: I will go and see her. But I would advise you to keep what you have told me to yourself for the time being.

REV JONES: I do not fear ridicule – I am blessed by God. Through this small child, God will speak to us all, and the whole world must know of the miracle of Sarah Jacob.

### TO THE EDITOR OF THE WELSHMAN
*(The letter that follows is Rev Jones' actual letter.)*

Sir – Allow me to invite the attention of your readers to a most extraordinary case – Sarah Jacob – a little girl of twelve years of age – daughter of Mr Evan Jacob – who has not partaken of a single grain of any kind of food whatever during the last sixteen months. She did occasionally swallow a few drops of water during the first few months of this period but now she does not even do that and yet continues in the possession of all her mental faculties. She is in this, and several other respects, a wonderful little girl. Medical men persist in saying that the thing is quite impossible but all the nearest neighbours entertain no doubt whatever on the subject and I am myself of the same opinion.

Would it be worth their while for medical men to make an investigation into the nature of this strange case?

*During the reading of the above letter, the chorus light the candles.*

### After the Letter

CHORUS: The Welsh Fasting Girl!

CHORUS: To the Welsh Fasting Girl!

CHORUS: Guide to Lletherneuadd.

*During the following, the bed is dressed with gifts of colourful shawls, books, flowers, etc. It has become a shrine with SARAH as the centrepiece.*

SARAH: Visitors
        Presents
        Clothes
        Prayer Books
        Hymn Books
        Poetry Books
        Story Books
        Picture Books
        Money
        Sixpences
        Shillings
        Florins
        Half Crowns
        Crowns
        And even two gold sovereigns
        From all over Wales...

CHORUS: And from England...

CHORUS: They come in their thousands...

CHORUS: To see the miracle...

CHORUS: Proclaimed by a Priest of the Church of England....

## Scene Five

DR DAVIES: Sarah Jacob, I've been hearing a lot about you lately. Do you remember me? I'm Dr Davies.

HANNAH: You remember Dr Davies came when you were ill with scarlet fever.

SARAH: Oh, yes.

DR DAVIES: That was quite some time ago now. Can you tell me how you are feeling today?

SARAH: I'm feeling quite well, thank you, Doctor.

DR DAVIES: Then why aren't you up and about with your brothers and sisters?

SARAH: Don't be silly, Doctor. I'm weak and I can't move my left leg, it's very stiff.

DR DAVIES: I see, let's take a look. Any aches or pains?

*He examines SARAH.*

HANNAH: Sometimes she gets a bad pain – just here.

*She indicates SARAH's stomach.*

DR DAVIES: Mrs Jacob?

*They turn down the covers.*

DR DAVIES: But it comes and goes does it? It's not there all the time?

SARAH: No.

DR DAVIES: And am I right in thinking she hasn't eaten for a number of weeks now?

HANNAH: That's quite right, Doctor.

DR DAVIES: And does she pass water?

SARAH: A little.

DR DAVIES: Do your bowels move?

SARAH: I don't think so. I was ill, but now I'm better. Y Doctor Mawr is looking after me.

DR DAVIES: Y Doctor Mawr?

SARAH: The Great Doctor. God himself.

DR DAVIES: When she was poorly, what were her symptoms? What happened?

SARAH: I had a cough, a bad cough, and I had blood in my mouth, and my hair fell out, and I got thinner and thinner.

DR DAVIES: Could you sit up for me please? I want to take a look at your back. Cough please, and again. Were you eating, Sarah?

SARAH: I tried to, Doctor, but it hurt.

DR DAVIES: Where did it hurt?

SARAH: All round here. (*She indicates her throat.*)

DR DAVIES: And what were you eating?

SARAH: Some apple, a little porridge, but it hurt in my throat, even a small sip of milk hurt.

DR DAVIES: Mrs Jacob, were you feeding her?

HANNAH: We tried to, Doctor, but she couldn't, so we stopped – it upset her too much.

DR DAVIES: So it's true that for some time now she hasn't taken any food or drink?

HANNAH: Yes.

SARAH: I'm not ill.

DR DAVIES: How are your brothers and sisters?

SARAH: They're very well, thank you.

HANNAH: Margaret's her favourite. She's always in here with her. Sarah reads to her from the Bible stories. She's teaching her to read.

*DR DAVIES takes SARAH's pulse.*

DR DAVIES: Are you fond of stories, Sarah?

SARAH: Oh yes.

DR DAVIES: Good. So you spend all your time in bed?

SARAH: Yes, Doctor.

HANNAH: She never gets up. Her father lifts her out when I've to change the linen.

DR DAVIES: I'd like to take a look at that leg. (*He pulls back the sheet to examine her leg.*)

SARAH: No. Noo. I can't. My leg. (*She has a violent fit then becomes very still.*)

DR DAVIES: Very well. It's alright, Sarah, I'm not going to touch you. Sarah? Sarah?

(*He leans close to her face. She opens her eyes and touches his cheek with the gloved hand.*)

SARAH: You've got a kind face, Doctor. Hasn't he, Mam?

DR DAVIES: Thank you.

SARAH: Have you got a wife?

DR DAVIES: Yes.

SARAH: What's her name?

DR DAVIES: Diana.

SARAH: (*Laughing*) Do you say your prayers?

DR DAVIES: Morning and night.

SARAH: I like you, Dr Davies.

DR DAVIES: I like you too, Sarah.

SARAH: I'm tired now, perhaps you'd like to call and see me again, Doctor.

DR DAVIES: I shall, you can be sure of that.

SARAH: Thank you.

*DR DAVIES and HANNAH leave SARAH. SARAH closes her eyes as if to sleep.*

DR DAVIES: Mrs Jacob, was she a child who enjoyed playing with others when she was... not as she is now?

HANNAH: She was never so active as the others, always thinking she was, quiet.

DR DAVIES: She has no bedsores. I would expect to see some, if she spent all her time in bed.

HANNAH: We sleep in the same room as her, Doctor, and we've never seen her move from her bed.

DR DAVIES: Quite so, Mrs Jacob, quite so. I should like to call and see her again.

HANNAH: You're very welcome.

DR DAVIES: Thank you. Goodbye.

*HANNAH goes to SARAH's bed.*

CHORUS: Lletherneuadd has become a place of pilgrimage...

CHORUS: Visitor after...

CHORUS: Visitor after...

CHORUS: Visitor...

CHORUS: Patiently, day after day...

CHORUS: They sit and wait...

CHORUS: In the kitchen...

CHORUS: Before the fire...

CHORUS: Waiting their turn to see...

CHORUS: Sarah Jacob.


## Scene Six

SARAH: Margaret, come here Margaret.

*MARGARET goes to SARAH, sits beside her on the bed. SARAH kisses her.*

SARAH: Shall I stroke your hair?

*MARGARET nods, SARAH strokes her hair.*

*After some time:*

MARGARET: (*Quietly, almost whispering*) My delight and thy delight...

SARAH: Walking like two angels white...

MARGARET/SARAH: In the garden of the night.

SARAH: Well done, Margaret. Have you learnt the other one yet?

*MARGARET shakes her head.*

SARAH: It's more difficult, isn't it? 'Twas midnight through the lattice wreath'd with woodbine, many a perfume...

MARGARET/SARAH: Breath'd...

SARAH: From plants that wake when others sleep, from timid jasmine buds that keep their odour to themselves all day, but when the sunlight dies...

MARGARET/SARAH: Away...

SARAH: Let the delicious secret out to every...

MARGARET/SARAH: Breeze that roams about! (*They laugh.*)

MARGARET: Can we do 'Jesus and His Supper' now, please?

SARAH: Alright.

*MARGARET leaves SARAH and returns with a little bread and some water.*

SARAH: (*Crumbling the bread*) And as they were eating He took bread and when He had blessed He broke it and gave to them and said, 'Take ye – this is my body.'

*She puts the bread in MARGARET's mouth.*

SARAH: Then He took a cup and when He had given thanks He gave to them and they all drank of it.

*She gives MARGARET the water to drink.*

SARAH: And He said unto them, 'This is the blood of my covenant...'

*MARGARET spits the water out.*

SARAH: 'Which is shed for many. Verily I say unto you I will no more drink of the fruit of the vine until that day when I drink it new in the Kingdom of God.'

*She gives the rest of the bread to MARGARET.*

SARAH: There – finish the bread, Margaret. Go on, eat it.

MARGARET: I don't want any more.

SARAH: Eat it.

MARGARET: I don't want it.

SARAH: Eat it.

MARGARET: No.

SARAH: Eat it.

MARGARET: No. You eat it. (*Trying to force bread into SARAH's mouth*) Go on, you eat...

SARAH: (*Struggling*) No, no, no – stop it, stop it... stop it.

MARGARET: (*Still trying to force her*) You eat, you eat, you eat...

SARAH: (*Struggling*) No, No. (*She goes into one of her fits – silence.*)

MARGARET: Sarah, Sarah, I'm sorry, Sarah. I'm sorry.

SARAH: I don't eat, do I, Margaret?

MARGARET: No.

SARAH: What don't I do?

MARGARET: You don't eat.

SARAH: What else don't I do?

MARGARET: You don't drink.

SARAH: (*Holding out some bread*) You swear on the Body of Christ – swear!

MARGARET: (*Taking the bread*) I swear. (*She eats it.*)

SARAH: Kiss me, Margaret.

*They kiss – their lips touching.*

SARAH: I do love you – I'm tired now.

*MARGARET kisses SARAH on the cheek, and leaves.*

SARAH: Verily I say unto you one of you shall betray me.

42

GOSSIP: It's a lot of attention for a little girl...

GOSSIP: I've been there...

GOSSIP: There are people in and out all the time...

GOSSIP: She looks really healthy...

GOSSIP: Plump face...

GOSSIP: Rosy cheeks...

GOSSIP: Well nourished if you ask me...

GOSSIP: I don't understand it...

GOSSIP: Someone said she's got hedgehog cells in her brain...

GOSSIP: She's headstrong...

GOSSIP: She's close to God. Spends all her time reading the Bible...

GOSSIP: And saying her prayers...

GOSSIP: What have hedgehogs got to do with it?

GOSSIP: I believe in her...

GOSSIP: I gave her a new prayer book...

GOSSIP: The vicar gave her a new Bible...

GOSSIP: He spends too much of his time with her...

GOSSIP: He's neglecting his other parishioners...

GOSSIP: What have hedgehogs got to do with it?

GOSSIP: Well, they sleep through the winter, don't they – they don't need to eat or drink, do they?

GOSSIP: Well, the family's certainly reaping a good harvest, whatever's going on...

DOUBTER: This stupidity and ignorance cannot be allowed to continue...

DOUBTER: It's blasphemy...

DOUBTER: Ignorance...

DOUBTER: The existence of a human being performing the acts ascribed to this girl for sixteen months without food is contradictory to an immense body of facts of various kinds...

DOUBTER: There are a number of strange stories in the world...

DOUBTER: And the matter of investigating them is very great...

DOUBTER: But once thoroughly investigated...

DOUBTER: The mystery commonly fades...

## Scene Seven

EVAN: I'd like to remind them, Vicar, that this fast had been going on for sixteen months before it was published to the world. It was your letter to the paper that started it.

REV JONES: My dear Evan, Hannah, I can understand you being upset by this idle gossip, but anyone who knows you, knows that you are honourable people.

EVAN: Until your letter, few people outside the parish had ever heard of Sarah. Now that they're pouring in to see her, are we to be held responsible?

HANNAH: You don't know what it's like, Vicar. Evan goes to the market and all he can hear is people talking – whispering, behind his back – never to his face.

REV JONES: I never imagined my letter would provoke quite this sort of response.

EVAN: I wish you'd never written it. Not everyone shares our faith in Sarah. They're saying we're frauds, liars – accusing me of cheating on the public.

HANNAH: It's not as if we ask them to leave presents or money.

EVAN: They're not for us anyway – leaving something behind when visiting the sick is quite usual, especially when it's a child. (*Pause.*) Most of those who come want to believe and leave with their faith strengthened, but these – these, these unbelievers – we have to prove to them that Sarah lives without food or drink. We could have her watched.

45

REV JONES: Evan...

EVAN: You're respected, a man of the cloth. If the suggestion were to come from you – a group of men who were honest and reliable who could watch her for as long as they thought necessary – then perhaps these doubters would have to accept that we are telling the truth.

REV JONES: Very well, Evan. I'll talk to Dr Davies.

WATCHER 1: Evan Edward Smith. I watched Sarah Jacob for two consecutive nights, and found nothing to suspect that food or drink was given to her by foul means.

WATCHER 2: Daniel Harries Davies. I found no indication that the child had anything to eat or drink.

WATCHER 3: James Harries Davies. I am positive that nothing has been given to the child with the exception of three drops of water once – used to moisten her lips.

WATCHER 4: Thomas Davies. I did my best to find out the secret for I believed there to be some secret connected with the affair. But after twelve days I am convinced that nothing was given to the girl.

GOSSIP: Daniel and James Harries Davies are Dr Davies' nephews...

GOSSIP: Evan Smith fell asleep, so I heard...

GOSSIP: And he's a close neighbour of the Jacobs...

GOSSIP: Thomas Davies is an old man – he's seventy-two!

GOSSIP: I don't think it proves anything...

GOSSIP: People will believe what they want to believe...

DOCTOR: To a medical man, this all appears to be very suspicious...

DOCTOR: I feel sure the explanation is hysteria...

DOCTOR: She is deceiving her parents...

DOCTOR: The girl is acting out a part...

DOCTOR: I can quite understand these poor simple people being easily deceived by their own child. The more especially as, in their ignorance, they seem to believe that there is a miracle and something superhuman in the case.


## Scene Eight

REV JONES: Pencader is turning into a battlefield.

DR DAVIES: Well, the evidence of the watch is just not sufficient to carry conviction in the scientific mind.

REV JONES: All this debate – 'Is she being fed or not?', 'The so-called Welsh Fasting Girl' – the honesty of the parents is continually called into question – my own reputation. I was sure that the watch would prove once and for all, that we are telling the truth.

DR DAVIES: I did warn you. Look, as a friend, I am prepared to accept that you and her parents firmly believe that the girl does not eat or drink. But as a doctor – a man of science...

REV JONES: I believe that nothing is impossible in the sight of God – the fast is a fact. There was a time when man found it impossible to believe the world to be round, but we now accept it as fact.

DR DAVIES: Alright, let us suppose that the girl is not eating or drinking...

REV JONES: Suppose! She isn't, Henry.

DR DAVIES: Let me finish. Even supposing that we accept that to be true, then there must be an explanation – a scientific explanation.

REV JONES: Such an explanation would make it no less a miracle.

DR DAVIES: But I need proof – incontrovertible proof. There must be a second watch – this time without taint of local bias. Fully professional watchers must be found. This time the case must be tested thoroughly and then and only then, my friend, would I be prepared to accept that this girl lives without food or drink.

REV JONES: And believe in the miracle?

DR DAVIES: Search for scientific enlightenment my friend – scientific enlightenment.

CHORUS: (*Chorally spoken by the three women*) At the request of several medical and other gentlemen in Wales, it has been arranged to send four nurses from Guy's Hospital,

London, to watch the girl who has lately been the cause of so much curiosity in the public mind...

CHORUS: (*All. Chant*)
    Is she being fed or not?
    Is she being fed or not?
    Is she being fed or not?
    Is she being fed or not?
    Is she being fed or not?
    Is she being fed or not?

EVAN: We would be extremely glad to have this matter thoroughly investigated.

## ACT TWO
### The Eight Day Watch

CHORUS: Evan Jacob, do you agree to provide a written legal guarantee sanctioning the necessary proceedings?

EVAN: I agree.

CHORUS: And that the duty of the nurses shall be to watch Sarah Jacob with a view to ascertaining whether she partakes of any kind of food and that special attention be directed towards movements of the bowel and bladder and that at the end of a fortnight the said nurses are to report upon the case to the committee?

EVAN: I agree.

CHORUS: And that the nearest medical practitioner shall watch the progress of the case and at sight of any serious symptoms of exhaustion act according to his judgement?

EVAN: I agree.

CHORUS: And that you, the parents, be not allowed to sleep in the same room as the girl and that you are searched before being allowed to approach her?

EVAN/HANNAH: We agree.

CHORUS: There will be three committees...

CHORUS: One to make arrangements for receiving the nurses...

CHORUS: Another medical committee to assist the nurses if necessary...

CHORUS: And another to receive the report of the nurses when the watching is done.

EVAN: I hope this enquiry will give satisfaction and put an end to the remarks that have been thrown in my teeth – accusing me of cheating on the public.

HANNAH: Our characters are as good as any from here to London.

CHORUS: London, Guy's Hospital...

CHORUS: Sister Nurse Elizabeth Clinch...

CHORUS: Nurse Sarah Palmer...

CHORUS: Nurse Sarah Attrick...

CHORUS: Nurse Anne Jones – Welsh-speaking...

CHORUS: Depart Paddington...

CHORUS: All aboard, London to Carmarthen, all aboard!

*The following is read to the rhythm of a steam engine starting off, and gathering speed, and eventually slowing down on arrival.*

CHORUS: Reading
         Didcot
         Swindon
         Bristol... (*Repeated*)

CHORUS: Cardiff
        Port Talbot
        Neath... (*Repeated*)

CHORUS: Swansea
        Llanelli... (*Repeated*)

CHORUS: Carmarthen... (*Repeated*)

CHORUS: All change for Pencader.

REV JONES: Reverend Evan Jones. I'm very pleased to meet you, Sister Clinch. Please allow me to attend to your luggage.

*SISTER CLINCH addresses the audience as if they are her colleagues who will be assisting her in carrying out 'The Watching'.*

CLINCH: Our duty is primarily and solely to watch whether or not she takes food. It is not to prevent her having it. If she asks for food or water to moisten her lips, we may give it to her. It is not our duty to keep food from the child, or prevent others from giving it to her. Only her father and mother may have contact with the child, and then only to shake hands. No other visitors are to be allowed near the bed. Two nurses shall be constantly awake to watch in the girl's room, night and day. Let the experiment begin!

*The CHORUS remove SARAH's head-dress, glove, and lace shawl; take the presents and quilt off the bed, leaving SARAH in her white nightdress, covered only with a plain white sheet.*

## Scene One
## The Calm after the Storm

CLINCH: Sarah had a very peaceful night – she slept for most of it.

HANNAH: She doesn't always sleep well.

CLINCH: She seems relaxed enough – with us.

HANNAH: She's very used to visitors.

CLINCH: So I gather. (*Pause.*) You do understand the reason we had...

HANNAH: Yes, yes, of course.

CLINCH: I don't want you to feel apprehensive in any way. It must be reassuring having Nurse Jones here – someone Sarah can speak to in Welsh.

HANNAH: Her English is very good.

CLINCH: Yes, yes, it's excellent.

HANNAH: She's very bright. She's always asking questions, always wanting to know everything about everything.

CLINCH: Is she close to her brothers and sisters?

HANNAH: Yes, but Margaret's her favourite.

CLINCH: She told me they spend quite a lot of time together.

HANNAH: Sarah's very good with her. She reads to her, tells her stories. Teaches her things. They're very close.

*Pause.*

CLINCH: Do you mind us being here?

HANNAH: Evan was very keen to go ahead with this watch – he's a proud man.

CLINCH: You are certain, then, that she isn't eating or drinking?

HANNAH: I think I would know if she was. (*Pause.*) You've never married?

CLINCH: No. I came close once – it wasn't meant to be.

HANNAH: Do you mind not having children?

CLINCH: I work a great deal with children.

HANNAH: Not the same as having your own though, is it?

CLINCH: Probably not. What are you making?

HANNAH: A lace collar.

CLINCH: For Margaret?

HANNAH: No, for Sarah – she likes pretty things.

CLINCH: Has she always enjoyed dressing up?

HANNAH: It's such a simple pleasure. It's one of the few things I can give her.

CLINCH: Was it your idea to put ribbons in her hair? Flowers?

HANNAH: When she was very ill, she lost her hair. I thought I'd disguise it. Then when she got better she liked them so much, I didn't like to take them away from her.

CLINCH: She looks quite healthy now.

HANNAH: Her faith sustains her. She has such remarkable faith. At times I'm quite envious.

CLINCH: Doesn't it frighten you? This strength she has.

HANNAH: She's just my little girl.

CLINCH: Has she always been special?

HANNAH: Yes, I suppose she has.

CLINCH: Isn't that difficult? What about the other children?

HANNAH: We've never treated her any differently from the others.

CLINCH: I just though that it must be difficult having such a demanding child.

HANNAH: I don't like that word.

*SARAH calls for her mother.*

SARAH: Mam, Mam.

*HANNAH stands and makes to go to SARAH. SISTER CLINCH stops her.*

CLINCH: No, I'll go. It'll be alright. It will soon be over.

*HANNAH returns to her stool. SISTER CLINCH goes to SARAH.*

## Scene Two

CLINCH: Now then, Sarah, what is it that you want?

SARAH: My feet are cold, Sister. The water jar is cold.

CLINCH: Let me see. Yes, you're quite right.

*SISTER CLINCH removes the bedsheet, takes out the stone jar, sees the top is loose and sheet slightly damp. She looks at SARAH and goes as though to refill the stone jar.*

SARAH: I'd like to read my poetry book now please – it's down there.

CLINCH: Here you are.

SARAH: Thank you. Would you like me to read to you, Sister?

CLINCH: I'd like that very much, Sarah.

SARAH: This one then.

*'Never Tell' – 12ᵗʰ century, Anon.*

The saplings of the green tipped birch
Draw my foot from bondage
Let no boy know your secret!

Oak saplings in the grove
Draw my foot from its chain
Tell no secret to a maid!

The leafy saplings of the oak
Draw my foot from prison
Tell no babbler a secret!

Briar shoots with berries on
Neither a blackbird on her nest
Nor a liar, are ever still.

CLINCH: You read very well, Sarah. You have a good strong voice. Do you understand the poem?

SARAH: Not really, I just like the sound of the words.

CLINCH: Do you miss Margaret? The little games you play together?

SARAH: Yes, but I'm happy to be with you nice ladies. You have a nice face.

CLINCH: So do you, Sarah.

SARAH: Do you have any children?

CLINCH: No, I'm not married. Would you like to marry one day – have children?

SARAH: I don't think it's meant for me Sister. (*Pause.*) I'm tired now.

*SARAH closes her eyes. SISTER CLINCH soothes her brow. SARAH falls asleep. SISTER CLINCH looks at HANNAH.*

CLINCH: She's asleep.

*She tidies, and takes SARAH's pulse, takes out her diary and writes.*

CLINCH: Day three.

*The waiting, watching, wondering sequence.*

*SISTER CLINCH watching SARAH, HANNAH rocking the cradle – like a clock ticking away the time, supported by MUSIC/LIGHTING.*

*This is a strictly choreographed movement sequence, which shows the waiting and watching: SISTER CLINCH checking SARAH's pulse, bathing her brow, straightening the bedclothes, writing in her diary and reassuring HANNAH; HANNAH rocking the cradle, doing her lacework, being searched by SISTER CLINCH before visiting, being prevented from embracing SARAH.*

*Whilst SISTER CLINCH watches, SARAH becomes restless. SISTER CLINCH goes to her, smooths her brow and watches.*

*The dream sequence.*

*SARAH rises from her bed and moves around the acting area, looking for MARGARET.*

SARAH: Margaret? Margaret? Where are you? Where are You? Play with me, Margaret. Where are you? Where are you, Margaret?

> My delight and thy delight.
> Walking like two Angels white.
> In the garden of the night.

Margaret, Margaret, answer me, answer me. Where are you? Where are you? It's a race, Margaret. I can't win on my own. Margaret, Margaret, Margaret. I'm cold, Margaret. I'm so cold. I'm cold, Mam. I'm cold. Mam – Mam, I'm cold.

*She returns to her bed. Restless in her sleep, she tosses and turns, coughing – her breathing is irregular. SISTER CLINCH soothes SARAH's brow. SARAH wakes.*

### Scene Three

CLINCH: Alright, Sarah, alright. It's just a dream, it's a dream, Sarah. (*Pause.*) Is there anything you want? Sarah?

*No reply.*

CLINCH: Anything at all?

*No reply.*

CLINCH: If there is, you can tell me. Tell me if you want anything.

*No reply.*

CLINCH: Would you like to read? Would you like to read to me Sarah?

*She passes SARAH her book. Feebly, SARAH begins to read 'God and His Church' by Morgan Llwyd, 1619-1659.*

SARAH: My God kiss my lips with thine,
    Sweeter is thy love than wine,
    Beloved of my soul art thou.

*Her voice trails away. SISTER CLINCH takes over the reading.*

CLINCH: A fragrant oil anoints thy head,
    Thy name quickeneth the dead,
    The true virgins love thee now.
    My pure church, my bride, my love,
    My sister and my gentle dove
    Hid where the cleft of rock allows,
    Thy face, thy voice discover thee,
    Welcome thou art to be with me,
    Who am the Lamb, and thou the Spouse.

*SARAH falls asleep. SISTER CLINCH checks her pulse, takes her temperature. HANNAH watches.*

CLINCH: It's alright, Mrs Jacob, I'm watching her. Everything will be alright.

*HANNAH returns to the cradle. The tick-tock rocking resumes. SISTER CLINCH sits and watches, takes out her diary.*

CLINCH: Day five. Patient restless, pulse rate exceedingly variable. Although I have done my best to reassure the parents, I have taken the precaution of sending for Dr Davies.

## Scene Four

DR DAVIES: Her pulse rate is normal, Sister.

CLINCH: Doctor, her pulse rate was not normal earlier.

DR DAVIES: Well, it is now.

CLINCH: You haven't seen her since the watch began. Don't you notice a change in her appearance?

DR DAVIES: There's nothing to worry about.

CLINCH: She's sleeping so much more – when she speaks her voice is weak. She's confused, restless. Shouldn't we be taking such symptoms more seriously?

DR DAVIES: She's in no immediate danger, Sister.

*He begins to leave. HANNAH stands, looks to him.*

DR DAVIES: It's alright, Mrs Jacob. No cause for alarm. There's no immediate cause for concern.

*He leaves. HANNAH looks at SARAH and SISTER CLINCH. The watching resumes. HANNAH rocking the cradle to and fro.*

## Scene Five

DR DAVIES: When were you last at Lletherneuadd?

REV JONES: Not since the first day of the watch.

DR DAVIES: How was Sarah?

REV JONES: You saw for yourself. Cheerful. A little apprehensive perhaps, at the prospect of...

DR DAVIES: I went to see her yesterday. I examined her.

REV JONES: And?

DR DAVIES: Her pulse was unsteady, her temperature high. Things are not as they should be. I must say, I am not happy with the situation.

REV JONES: Henry, are you trying to tell me that the child might be failing?

DR DAVIES: I can't be sure...

REV JONES: Well, you examined her...

DR DAVIES: I think the watch should be called off.

REV JONES: Do you realise the implications of what you are suggesting? We'll be totally discredited – everything that was said about Sarah, her parents, myself, will be confirmed!

DR DAVIES: Be that as it may, I am not prepared to risk the girl's life further.

REV JONES: But you were the one who wanted this watch. You were the one who wanted incontrovertible proof.

DR DAVIES: And now I see how mistaken I was – to have even considered the possibility that a human being can live without nourishment. This experiment must end now.

REV JONES: Experiment, experiment – is that all the child is to you?

DR DAVIES: This watch must be called off!

REV JONES: But the parents – their honesty, the testimony of so many people.

DR DAVIES: As you are not prepared to accept my judgement in this matter, you leave me with no alternative but to resign from the Watch Committee. And let me tell you, I accept no further responsibility for the fate of this girl.

REV JONES: Henry, please, it's been but six days. Perhaps she's...

DR DAVIES: Go and see for yourself and then tell me if you still believe in miracles! (*Exits.*)

## Scene Six

*HANNAH rocking the cradle, SISTER CLINCH pacing.*

CLINCH: Mrs Jacob?

HANNAH: Yes?

CLINCH: There is something I must ask you. Are you absolutely certain that at no time during the past two years Sarah did not eat or drink? Mrs Jacob, when I arrived here she appeared to be healthy but during these past six days I have seen a change...

HANNAH: She's tired – the strange circumstances.

CLINCH: I have seen a marked change in her appearance.

HANNAH: You heard what the doctor said and, with all respect, Sister Clinch, I prefer to accept the doctor's opinion.

CLINCH: Mrs Jacob, I have watched her. I have watched your daughter deteriorate, and I am helpless to do anything about it. Look at her, look at her now. Logic, reason, tells me that she must have been eating prior to this watch – nourishment of which she is now deprived. Nourishment which I am forbidden to give her and for which she is no longer capable of asking.

HANNAH: Sarah has not eaten or had anything to drink for two years.

CLINCH: Can you be absolutely certain? Margaret, perhaps? Might Margaret have been feeding her? At night? What about when you and your husband and the household slept? Mrs Jacob, please – look at her, look at her. Can't you see she's slipping further and further away from us?

HANNAH: She's been ill before. She got better. Her faith, our faith, sustains her. She's ill, but she'll get better.

CLINCH: She is not ill, she is dying. Your daughter is dying. Please, call an end to this watch.

HANNAH: No! Evan... (*pause*) Evan gave his word.

CLINCH: I am bound by my duty, you are her mother.

*EVAN enters. SISTER CLINCH looks at him, gives one last imploring look to HANNAH, then returns to SARAH. EVAN looks at SISTER CLINCH and HANNAH, then sits. HANNAH rocks the cradle to and fro. Watching. Waiting.*


## Scene Seven

*REV JONES goes to SARAH's bedside. He looks at her, then at SISTER CLINCH. He turns, HANNAH rises, they look at each other. He goes to HANNAH and EVAN.*

REV JONES: She's asleep.

*Silence. HANNAH and REV JONES exchange glances. He paces the room.*

EVAN: Sit down, Vicar, why don't you?

REV JONES: (*Remains standing*) She doesn't look at all well, Evan.

EVAN: She's asleep, you said. Can't tell what she is or isn't when she's asleep.

REV JONES: She's so pale.

EVAN: Why don't you sit down, Vicar.

REV JONES: I haven't seen her look this way before – in all the time that I've been visiting her...

EVAN: The doctor's been. He says there's no cause for concern. Sit down, Hannah.

65

REV JONES: I think she's failing, Evan.

EVAN: Failing – failing, Vicar. Sit down, Hannah!

HANNAH sits.

REV JONES: (*To Hannah*) How long has she been like this?

EVAN: Like what?

REV JONES: In God's name, Evan – like this.

EVAN: She was ill before – she recovered. She'll recover again.

REV JONES: When I spoke to Dr Davies yesterday he told me he wants this watch called off.

EVAN: God Almighty is watching over Sarah now...

REV JONES: Evan, please...

EVAN: Just as He always has.

REV JONES: I'm telling you that Dr Davies believes she may be dying – he will accept no further responsibility for her. Please, Evan, call off the watch.

EVAN: Never. I have faith – my faith will be rewarded.

REV JONES: Evan, look at her – your child is dying, she needs to eat. Please give her some milk – anything.

EVAN: Faith is a gift from God, and only He knows who has it. Do you still have yours or not?

REV JONES: I...

EVAN: If you have lost your faith then you feed her, but we shall not – I took an oath.

HANNAH: Please, Evan...

EVAN: I took an oath – I swore to Sarah that I would neither offer nor give her food or drink unless she asked.

REV JONES: She can't ask, Evan – she's beyond that.

*HANNAH returns to her rocking.*

EVAN: Sarah will recover, she will be restored to us. I have faith, I believe.

REV JONES: I beg you, Evan, one last time, before it's too late, call off this watch.

EVAN: Not for the world.

*REV JONES leaves. HANNAH rocking to and fro. EVAN sits, immovable.*

CLINCH: Day eight. I have implored the parents to give the child brandy and water, but to no avail. I now fear the outcome is inevitable – the child will die.

HANNAH: (*Almost inaudible, growing in volume*)
    Call off the watch
    Call off the watch

Call off the watch
Call off the watch
Call off the watch
Call off the watch...

EVAN: Quiet, woman. If you must speak, speak to God.

HANNAH: Look at her, Evan – look at her.

EVAN: She's been like this before.

HANNAH: Please, Evan...

EVAN: Quiet, Hannah!

HANNAH: She's failing.

EVAN: Failing! She will not fail. God has watched over her. We must be resolute in our faith.

HANNAH: She's only flesh and blood, Evan. Look at her.

EVAN: Quiet!

HANNAH: What if we were wrong?

EVAN: Quiet!

HANNAH: What if we were wrong?

EVAN: We have not been wrong.

HANNAH: Can we be certain?

EVAN: Quiet!

HANNAH: What... what if... she... she... was eating... secretly... somehow... and now... she's dying.

*EVAN forces HANNAH to her knees.*

EVAN: Pray – pray for the restoration of your faith. If Sarah should die I will blame you – for your lack of faith.

HANNAH: She needs feeding, Evan.

EVAN: She needs our prayers.

HANNAH: She needs more than our prayers.

EVAN: God is testing us. We must be strong. You must be strong.

HANNAH: For God's sake, Evan, let me feed her.

EVAN: No!

HANNAH: She must have been eating at night. Margaret – while we were asleep, when they were playing.

EVAN: Quiet!

HANNAH: Please, Evan, let me feed her.

EVAN: No!

HANNAH: Before it's too late.

*HANNAH grabs the jug, runs to SARAH's bedside. It's too late – SARAH is dead.*

EVAN: Hannah!

*SISTER CLINCH draws the sheet over SARAH's face.*

HANNAH: (*Screams*) No!

EVAN: Sarah? Sarah? Sarah? (*Throws himself on the bed.*) Sarah....

*The End.*

*During the run of performances the following was added as a postscript.*

CLINCH: Sarah Jacob died on 17th December 1869. Evan and Hannah Jacob were charged with the manslaughter of their daughter by causing her death through their culpable abstention from giving her food. Found guilty, Evan was imprisoned and kept to hard labour for twelve calendar months. Hannah was imprisoned and kept to hard labour for six calendar months. The medical profession were totally exonerated. The vicar recognised that they were sadder but not much wiser men.

# Wishful Thinking

**Hijinx Theatre**

First performed at Crownbridge Gateway Club
15 February 1990.

Cast:

| | | |
|---|---|---|
| Michelle | – | Erica Eirian |
| Barbara | – | Glenys Evans |
| Rachel | – | Gaynor Lougher |

Flute music performed by Juliet Marsh.

Creative Team:

| | | |
|---|---|---|
| Director | – | Rosamunde Hutt |
| Designer | – | Annette Scriven |
| Music | – | Matthew Bailey |
| Assistant Director | – | Valerie Lucas |
| Lighting Designer Stage Manager | – | Juliet Marsh |

A play for adults with learning difficulties and the important people in their lives. Devised by Matthew Bailey, Erica Eirian, Glenys Evans, Rosamunde Hutt, Gaynor Lougher, Valerie Lucas, and Annette Scriven.

# Prologue

*MICHELLE puts on a record of Patsy Cline's 'I Fall to Pieces'.*
*She dances. She is waiting for Barbara to arrive. She sings along;*
*dances with an imaginary man. When the song ends, she turns off the*
*record. BARBARA enters, carrying a box.*

BARBARA: I'm home!

MICHELLE: (*Looking up*) Barbara!

BARBARA: (*Puts down box*) All right?

MICHELLE: Yes.

BARBARA: Anyone call?

MICHELLE: No.

*BARBARA takes off her coat. She unwraps a mop, then folds the*
*paper and puts it in the box. She takes out a magazine and a packet*
*of sweets. MICHELLE holds out packet of sweets.*

BARBARA: Look what I've got.

MICHELLE: (*Taking sweeets*) Is it teatime yet?

BARBARA: Give me five minutes.

## Scene One
## It's too Hot to Cuddle, Love

*BARBARA sits, reading her magazine. MICHELLE puts on the*
*record, then lies face down, kicking her legs in time to the music.*

73

*After half a verse, she puts the song back to the beginning, and turns the volume up. BARBARA groans. MICHELLE stands, as though in someone's arms. After half a verse, MICHELLE puts the stylus back to the beginning of the record, and again turns the volume up. BARBARA turns the volume down.*

BARBARA: Just a bit. Just a bit.

*MICHELLE turns the volume up. BARBARA turns the record player off.*

MICHELLE : You've spoilt it now.

BARBARA: This is my time.

MICHELLE: I'll have it on very quietly, alright.

*MICHELLE turns the record player on, at almost full volume. After half a verse, she puts it back to the beginning.*

BARBARA: Finished? Have you finished?

MICHELLE: (*Putting on record*) Just once more.

*BARBARA turns the record player off.*

BARBARA: No.

MICHELLE: (*Turns it on*) Just once more.

BARBARA: (*Turns it off*) No.

MICHELLE: (*Turns it on*) Please.

BARBARA: (*Turns it off*) No Michelle.

MICHELLE: (*Turns it on*) Please.

*BARBARA makes to leave.*

MICHELLE : Where are you going? Don't go out, don't go out, don't go out. Sorry.

*MICHELLE moves towards BARBARA, and BARBARA cuddles her, then breaks the embrace.*

BARBARA: It's too hot to cuddle, love.

*MICHELLE offers sweets to BARBARA. BARBARA makes a secret sign. MICHELLE copies.*

BARBARA: I wish someone would call, don't you? Shall we go and see Sheila at Marks and Sparks?

MICHELLE: What's today?

BARBARA: Tuesday.

MICHELLE: We go and see Sheila on Wednesdays.

*DUET:*

| *BARBARA:* | *MICHELLE:* |
|---|---|
| It's too hot | It's too hot |
| In the house | In the house |
| Not a breath of air | Not a breath of air |
| Heat and closeness | Heat and closeness |
| Everywhere | Everywhere |
| And time is ticking on | ... |
| *(Canon)* | And time is ticking on |

*Moves to the mop and bucket.*

| | |
|---|---|
| In our house | Safe and sure |
| Which we share | In our house |
| Though we're only two | Living here is fun |
| I often feel it's much too small | She's my sister and my friend |
| I'm never on my own | We always do the same |

*Mops the floor.*

| | |
|---|---|
| Like a dance | It's what I know |
| I can't stop | Feeling safe |
| Hardly space to breathe | Every day is planned |
| Cleaning, scrubbing, wiping down | Everything's in order here |
| And always more to do | It's always been like that |

*Stands.*

| | |
|---|---|
| It's too hot | It's too hot |
| In the house | In the house |
| Not a breath of air | Not a breath of air |
| Heat and closeness | Heat and closeness |
| Everywhere | Everywhere |
| | ... |
| | And time is ticking on |

*RACHEL enters.*

*Mops.*

| | |
|---|---|
| She heads off in a sulk | It's what I know |
| It happens more and more | Feeling safe |
| Hides out in her room | She's been in my room |

76

| | |
|---|---|
| Treats me like her enemy | Snooping around and moving things |
| She doesn't speak for days | It's not a secret place |
| | |
| I love her (*faces away*) | She loves me (*faces away*) |
| Though it's hard | In her way |
| How much can I take? | She's been very kind to me |
| (Yet I) love her, | (But it's) not |
| Love her so | It's not the same |
| | |
| What I want | I want to do |
| In my heart | What we do |
| Is not to have to clean | In our normal way |
| Not to have to organise | Nothing's ever going to |
| To throw the clock away | Change |
| ... | ... |

*BARBARA and MICHELLE face each other. RACHEL stands.*

BARBARA/MICHELLE: Pain and joy...

RACHEL: (*Spoken*) My two sisters...

BARBARA/MICHELLE: Love and life...

RACHEL: (*Spoken*) I love them both so much...

BARBARA/MICHELLE: The dance that will not end...

RACHEL: (*Spoken*) Barbara and Michelle...

BARBARA/MICHELLE: A song of longing and of fear...

RACHEL: (*Spoken*) I'm the one that got away.

BARBARA/MICHELLE: The ties that tear and bind.

*BARBARA and MICHELLE embrace. RACHEL stands behind them.*

RACHEL: (*Spoken*) My two sisters: Barbara and Michelle.

## Scene Two
## Amazing Grace

*BARBARA sits. MICHELLE kneels, cuddling her.*

BARBARA: I'm going to bed.

MICHELLE: No, no, don't go to bed yet.

BARBARA: Can't I go to bed if I'm tired?

MICHELLE: It's the news – we always watch the news and then we watch 'Cagney and Lacey'.

BARBARA: Look, I've watched the one o'clock, six o'clock, nine o'clock news. It's depressing. I don't want to watch the news.

MICHELLE: But we always watch the news and then we always watch 'Cagney and Lacey'.

BARBARA: Are you going to sulk if I go to bed?

MICHELLE: (*Releasing her*) No.

BARBARA: I'm going to bed.

MICHELLE: (*Stops her*) No.

BARBARA: Hey, Michelle (*Holds out hands*). Which hand – this one or this one?

*MICHELLE takes sweet.*

BARBARA: Don't make a fuss, Michelle. Bring me a cup of tea in the morning.

MICHELLE: Alright. And then you can have a wash and clean your teeth...

BARBARA: And them I'm going to work. Good night.

MICHELLE: (*Stops her*) But what about 'Cagney and Lacey'?

BARBARA: You can tell me what happens. (*Sits.*)

MICHELLE: Barbara Barbara Barbara Barbara.

BARBARA: I'm asleep.

MICHELLE: No you're not.

*BARBARA Rises.*

MICHELLE: Do you want some hot chocolate?

BARBARA: (*Rising*) Cup of tea in the morning, thank you.

MICHELLE: (*Stops her*) Do you want some water?

BARBARA: Good night.

MICHELLE: (*Stopping her*) Do you want to hear my record?

BARBARA: Good night.

MICHELLE: But we always watch 'Cagney and Lacey'.

BARBARA: See my lips move? I'm saying two words: 'good' and 'night'.

MICHELLE: What time shall we get up in the a.m.? Tell me that and I'll let you go.

BARBARA: Eight o'clock a.m..

MICHELLE: Right, let's say you get up at eight o'clock a.m. and then you can have a wash and then you can clean your teeth and I can do the washing up and then you can go to work and then when you come back we can have our dinner and then we can...

*BARBARA pretends to choke and fall over.*

MICHELLE: Go and do 'the big shop' at Tesco's in Culverhouse Cross and then we can have a light snack in the coffeeshop. Barbara?

BARBARA: I'm dead.

MICHELLE: Shall I take your shoes off?

*MICHELLE unties BARBARA's shoes.*

MICHELLE: If you didn't have me you wouldn't know what to do, would you – see. I'll get you ready for bed.

*BARBARA sings 'Amazing Grace'.*

MICHELLE: Barbara, you wouldn't know what to do without me, see.

*MICHELLE pulls BARBARA up.*

MICHELLE: So! Tomorrow afternoon...

MICHELLE/BARBARA: We'll do 'the big shop' at Tesco's on Culverhouse Cross...

MICHELLE: And then in the evening we'll go to our social club and you can have a gin and tonic and I'll have...

MICHELLE/BARBARA: Half a lager with a lemonade top.

BARBARA: And this time next week we can go to the club with Rachel!

MICHELLE: Yes – Rachel will be home. What will we do on Saturday, Barbara? What time will we get up in the a.m.?

BARBARA: We'll get up at dinner time.

MICHELLE: No, no. I'll bring you a cup of tea at – let's say a quarter past nine a.m. and then you can have a wash and then you can clean your teeth and...

BARBARA: And read the papers in a relaxed way.

MICHELLE: Let's say we have dinner at, say, ten past one and let's say we finish by twenty-five to two we can wash and dry up by say two and then we can get a bus at...

BARBARA: There's one every twenty minutes...

MICHELLE: You sure?

BARBARA: Yes.

MICHELLE: Then we can go to the museum and have tea in the tea shop. There – shall I have a rock cake or a Welsh cake?

BARBARA: A rock cake with jam.

MICHELLE: And then we'll come home and get a video out.

BARBARA: Yes.

MICHELLE: 'Roger Rabbit'?

BARBARA: No. 'Indiana Jones and the Temple of Doom'.

MICHELLE: Not Harrison Ford again!

BARBARA/MICHELLE: Pain and joy...

RACHEL: (*Spoken*) My two sisters.

BARBARA/MICHELLE: Love and life...

RACHEL: (*Spoken*) They live in a world of their own.

BARBARA/MICHELLE: The dance that will not end.

RACHEL: (*Spoken*) I wish I was closer to them.

BARBARA/MICHELLE: A song of longing and of fear.

RACHEL: (*Spoken*) I wish I knew what they needed.

BARBARA/MICHELLE: The ties that tear and bind.

RACHEL: (*Spoken*) I wish they could be at peace.

### Scene Three
### Look Me in the Eyes

BARBARA: Tell me the truth, Michelle. The truth about the course.

*MICHELLE collects paper and envelopes. She sits, stuffing envelopes.*

BARBARA: (*Kneels, facing her*) You didn't go, did you?

MICHELLE: I did.

BARBARA: Look me in the eyes! Look me in the eyes! I wanted you to go on that course.

MICHELLE: I did go.

BARBARA: I'm not like Mum. I'm not going to let you slide out of doing things.

MICHELLE: They can hear you next door.

BARBARA: Look me in the eyes! (*She takes away the envelopes.*) Look me in the eyes!

MICHELLE: No! I did go!

BARBARA: Well tell me about it then. What did you do on the course?

MICHELLE: I did go! I did go!

BARBARA: You couldn't have been. Doris says she saw you. In town. In the record shop. In the morning. That's when you should have been on the course.

MICHELLE: (*Pacing*) I did go! I did go! I did go!

BARBARA: Did you get through the door? Did you get through the door, Michelle?

MICHELLE: Leave me alone!

*BARBARA confronts MICHELLE. MICHELLE turns away.*

MICHELLE: I did go!

BARBARA: Do you think Doris would lie to me? Michelle, we're sisters. I tell you everything. Please, tell me what happened. You promised you'd go.

MICHELLE: You wouldn't want to go on it.

BARBARA: I'd have come with you.

MICHELLE: I have to go on my own.

BARBARA: It was only three mornings. Three mornings. And you didn't go.

MICHELLE: I went on Monday.

BARBARA: And I made you sandwiches every day.

MICHELLE : I ate them.

BARBARA: You have got to do something.

MICHELLE: It made me sick.

BARBARA: You've got to do something.

MICHELLE: I couldn't face it.

BARBARA: You've got to do things without me.

MICHELLE: Why? You won't make me go, will you?

*Beat.*

MICHELLE: It's Rachel.

BARBARA: It can't be Rachel.

MICHELLE: She's early.

BARBARA: Michelle, open the door. (*Tidies away paper.*) Michelle, it's your sister. Open the door.

*RACHEL enters. They look at her.*

BARBARA: Valaya – migayama voyomo layaba vigo.

BARBARA/MICHELLE: Lamakar – veecolomo – vagassar – vee-a – viralar ma-ee-ehgala.

85

*RACHEL takes one step in.*

ALL: Valaya – migayama voyomo layaba vigo lamakar veecolomo vagassar. (*They hold hands, in a circle.*) Valaya – migayama voyomo layaba vigo lamakar veecolomo vagassar vee-a – viralar maee-ehgala. (*They break pose, take one step back. Look.*) Zeelago mirimiri lavigoyo zilamar zayabigar laya zilago ma-ee-eh la-do-si la-do-si...

*RACHEL tries to catch MICHELLE's eye.*

ALL: Zeelago mirimiri lavi-goyo zilamar zayabigar laya zilago ma-ee-eh la-do-si la-do-si.

### Scene Four
### Rachel's Return

BARBARA: Let me help you. Michelle, get a chair for Rachel.

*MICHELLE brings a chair. RACHEL sits, takes a poster from her rucksack and gives it to MICHELLE.*

RACHEL: This is for your room.

BARBARA: I'll take your bag. I'll take this to your room.

MICHELLE: Shall I help you with your coat?

*MICHELLE helps RACHEL off with her coat, dumps it on the floor. BARBARA takes coat and hangs it.*

BARBARA: I've put fresh flowers in your room.

MICHELLE : She's put fresh flowers in your room.

*BARBARA and MICHELLE sit and look at RACHEL.*

BARBARA: Now, would you like a cup of tea?

RACHEL: No thanks. Not at the moment.

MICHELLE: We went to Tesco's on Cowbridge Road East this morning to get things for our meal. Usually we go to Tesco's at Culverhouse Cross on a Thursday afternoon to do a 'big shop'.

BARBARA: Every Thursday.

MICHELLE: But as you were coming we thought we better go to Tesco's on Cowbridge Road East because it's nearer. Barbara chose the food and I chose the drinks. We got you a Guinness because it's full of goodness – that was my idea, wasn't it Barbara?

BARBARA: Yes, that was Michelle's idea.

MICHELLE: And I chose a ready-mixed gin and tonic for Barbara because that's her tipple – isn't it, Barbara?

BARBARA: Yes, I do like a gin and tonic now and then.

MICHELLE: And I chose a Diet Pepsi for me. We've got three packets of low-fat crisps, three low-fat salads, three different low-fat cheeses and three special chocolates – we've got three of everything because there's three of us now.

BARBARA: Yes, that's right Michelle.

MICHELLE: We went in a taxi there and back and we counted fourteen satellite dishes, didn't we Barbara?

BARBARA: Yes, that's enough, Michelle. I want to talk to Rachel.

*BARBARA draws her chair forward. MICHELLE copies.*

MICHELLE: When are you going back?

RACHEL: I'm not sure.

MICHELLE: Well, we'll have to know because of planning and organising everything.

BARBARA: Ssh, Michelle. (*She moves closer to RACHEL.*) You stay as long as you need.

MICHELLE: (*Moves closer*) Well, we'll need to know.

BARBARA: (*Moves closer*) Sssh, sssh.

MICHELLE: Don't. (*Moves closer.*) We'll all have to go to Tesco's at Culverhouse Cross on Thursday afternoon to do 'the big shop'. Usually we go to the coffeeshop...

BARBARA: Mich, Rachel doesn't want to hear about 'the big shop' at Culverhouse Cross.

MICHELLE: Why not? We like going there and to the coffeeshop. Usually we have...

BARBARA: Ssh, ssh.

MICHELLE: Don't! What are you ssshing for?

88

BARBARA: Rachel's just arrived!

*Beat.*

MICHELLE: Are you going to have your baby here?

RACHEL: Maybe.

MICHELLE: Blimey! You'll have to tell us what you like to eat. Usually we have everything low-fat. Low-fat crisps, low-fat cheese, low-fat spread.... We do. We like watching telly. We like 'Blockbusters'...

RACHEL: 'Give us a "G", Bob!'

MICHELLE: And 'Blankety Blank' and 'Blind Date' and 'Coronation Street'...

BARBARA: And sheep trails and dog trails...

MICHELLE: And 'EastEnders' and...

*MICHELLE hums 'Cagney and Lacey' theme.*

BARBARA: 'Cagney and Lacey'.

MICHELLE: She's Cagney and I'm Lacey.

*MICHELLE hums.*

BARBARA: That's enough Michelle, that's enough.

MICHELLE: And we like 'Neighbours'...

BARBARA: I don't like 'Neighbours'.

MICHELLE: You do.

BARBARA: I don't, Rachel.

MICHELLE: She does, Rachel.

| BARBARA: | MICHELLE: |
|---|---|
| Hey, Rachel, we've got new neighbours – yuppies. They've made some changes. | Rachel, she does. Why are you saying you don't like 'Neighbours'? We always watch it together. |
| Everything's stripped out, put back in Rachel, I don't like 'Neighbours' Rachel, I don't like 'Neighbours'... | Rachel, we always watch it together Rachel, she does Rachel, she does... |

RACHEL: I can't hear you both at once.

*Beat.*

MICHELLE: Do you like 'Neighbours', Rachel?

*RACHEL rises.*

RACHEL: My two sisters. I want to work miracles for them. They forget I'm only Rachel. I wish I knew what they wanted. Where do we start?

## Scene Five
## The Trip Out

RACHEL: We're going out. (*She gets their coats.*)

BARBARA: We're going out.

*BARBARA and RACHEL put on their coats. BARBARA helps MICHELLE with hers, buttons it for her.*

BARBARA: We're going out.

RACHEL: We're going out.

*BARBARA picks up an umbrella and opens it. All three walk to the shops. BARBARA closes umbrella. They enter a shopping arcade.*

MICHELLE: It's never going to stop raining. It's a good job we came in here. Otherwise everyone would be in a bad mood.

RACHEL: Never mind. We'll go shopping.

BARBARA: I'm thinking of having driving lessons.

RACHEL: If Robbie and I bought a car you could drive it when he's away on ship.

*MICHELLE pushes between RACHEL and BARBARA.*

MICHELLE: We don't need a car. We use taxis and we only use two taxis a week to do 'the big shop' at Culverhouse Cross.

RACHEL: But think of all the other things you could do.

91

BARBARA: There's more to life than 'the big shop' at Culverhouse Cross, Michelle. (*To RACHEL*) If I could drive, I'd look for another job.

RACHEL: What kind of job?

MICHELLE: Two taxis a week – two times fifty-two – that's a hundred and four taxis a year.

BARBARA: I'd go back to training again. At Marks and Sparks.

MICHELLE: Let's say three pound each – hang on – that's three hundred and twelve pounds a year.

BARBARA: I'd have to go on courses. If you were nearby, she could go and stay with you...

RACHEL: After the baby's born.

MICHELLE: Oi, oi. It's much cheaper to have two taxis a week than to have a car.

RACHEL: If we had a car we could go anywhere, anytime – daytrips, with the baby...

BARBARA: So what would you do if I had driving lessons?

MICHELLE: What day would you have them?

BARBARA: Monday afternoons.

MICHELLE: That's all right. I do the ironing on Monday afternoons. I like ironing all the flat things. I do the towels and the tea towels...

BARBARA: What about Wednesdays?

MICHELLE: Ssh, I'm telling Rachel something. I do the pillowcases and the handkerchiefs...

BARBARA: She'll never agree to me having driving lessons.

RACHEL: She said yes.

MICHELLE: And sometimes I do the sheets.

BARBARA: You don't do anything unless I push you, do you?

MICHELLE: I do.

BARBARA: Only if I stand over you.

MICHELLE: I do do things. I do. I do. I do.

RACHEL : I've had enough. I'm off to the shops.

MICHELLE: Don't go.

RACHEL: (*Turns*) The pair of you go on and on and on.

MICHELLE: Don't go.

RACHEL: I'll see you in Boots, Mich.

*RACHEL exits. MICHELLE and BARBARA stand at the door.*

MICHELLE: Don't go.

BARBARA: We're always like this.

*Silence.*

MICHELLE: She'll be in a bad mood now. It's all your fault. You big bossy old bag.

BARBARA: I want to have my driving lessons. I wanted you to say yes in front of Rachel so you'd stick to it.

MICHELLE: I did. I did.

BARBARA: Sorry.

MICHELLE: Sorry. She'll be in a bad mood now.

BARBARA: Never mind. I'll get round Rach.

*BARBARA puts her arms around MICHELLE's shoulders. They turn to leave. MICHELLE breaks away. RACHEL enters. RACHEL offers a lipstick to MICHELLE, and then to BARBARA. They try lipstick on their hands.*

RACHEL: Let's go.

BARBARA: (*Offers umbrella*) I'll see you back at home.

MICHELLE: We're going shopping.

*RACHEL and MICHELLE walk away. BARBARA watches, then takes off her coat and hangs it. She puts a record on the record player – Brahms. She takes out a scarf from her rucksack and tries it on. She dances with it, then lies on the floor.*

## Scene Six
## Conflict – Barbara's Explosion

*RACHEL and MICHELLE enter, carrying a rug in a Marks and Spencer bag. They look at the rucksack, the scarf, and BARBARA on floor. RACHEL coughs, BARBARA opens her eyes.*

RACHEL: Please. Don't let us disturb you.

*BARBARA stands, and turns the record player off. She begins mopping the floor. RACHEL and MICHELLE lay the rug on the floor, and wait expectantly.*

BARBARA: Very nice, but it's not my taste. If I was choosing, I wouldn't have chosen that one. (*She drags the rug to centre left*). You trip over a rug. Lino's safer.

*RACHEL replaces the rug.*

RACHEL: If you give it a chance, you might like it.

*RACHEL and MICHELLE exchange looks. Emphatically, BARBARA removes rug to centre left.*

BARBARA: If you wanted to make changes, Rachel, you should have asked me first.

*RACHEL and BARBARA exchange looks. MICHELLE replaces rug.*

MICHELLE: It's nice.

*RACHEL and BARBARA look at her. MICHELLE sits.*

BARBARA: If you wanted to throw your money about, you could have... bought me a better mop.

*BARBARA dumps the rug on RACHEL's and MICHELLE's laps.*

BARBARA: And don't get used to it – it's going back.

*RACHEL and MICHELLE place rug on floor and firmly plant their feet on it. BARBARA mops toward them.*

BARBARA: Can't you see what I'm doing? Can you move it please? I can give you a list of a hundred things that need doing in this house – the pair of you – sitting there.

*BARBARA dumps her rucksack and scarf on rug.*

RACHEL: Do you want a cup of tea, Barbara?

*BARBARA mops to either side of rug.*

BARBARA: No thank you. Can you move it please? Can you move it please?

MICHELLE: You've done that bit.

RACHEL: And there's another bit you've done.

MICHELLE: And there.

*RACHEL and MICHELLE giggle. MICHELLE continues until start of BARBARA's aria.*

BARBARA: It's not funny! I'm not laughing. I am trying to clean the floor.

RACHEL: Barbara, nobody's making you clean the floor.

BARBARA: Rachel, somebody's got to do it! This was my time! (*She throws her scarf and rucksack one way, and the rug next to them.*) This was my time! (*She leans on the mop, and looks away from them.*)

BARBARA: (*Sings*) This is not a holiday for me, you know.
It's every day of my life.
Stuck here with Michelle,
two stuffed canaries asleep in a cage.
Nothing is happening, nothing is changing.
I need a change.

*BARBARA faces MICHELLE and RACHEL*

BARBARA: (*Sings*) I want one chance to be myself.
Out and about on my own.
I want to choose the way I'm living
Free to choose what I want to do
But then where would Michelle be?

*MICHELLE rises. BARBARA drops her mop.*

BARBARA: (*Sings*) Rachel, I've been waiting for you
I'm still waiting for you to give me a break
From Michelle
(*Shouts*) Telly, telly, telly
morning, noon and night!
AARGH!
Six years of my life!

RACHEL: Six years. The first time we've really spoken for six years. I can't work miracles, Barbara. (*She rises.*) I'm only Rachel.

*RACHEL and BARBARA embrace. RACHEL makes their secret sign. BARBARA copies. BARBARA picks up her scarf, and winds it around her head. They both laugh. RACHEL places the rug in a bag, and shrugs.*

## Scene Seven
## The Moment of Despair

BARBARA: (*Listening at the door*) 'Chelle, say something. 'Chelle, say something.

*Beat.*

BARBARA: 'Chelle, say something. Michelle, please say something. Put your record on. (*Sings 'I Fall to Pieces'.*) 'Chelle, say something. Please. I'm going out to get some doughnuts in a minute. Coming? Nice doughnuts. One for you, one for me. And one for Rachel. Speak to me, please.

*Beat.*

BARBARA: (*To Rachel*) She's not daft. Do you know, she's got a packet of Petit Beurres, the bourbons, and my After Eights that I bought to give the neighbours. I'm sorry, I don't like who I'm becoming.

RACHEL: Sssh, sssh.

*RACHEL smiles, and seats BARBARA in a chair. MICHELLE stands, as if in another room. RACHEL sits, filing her nails and whistling the theme tune from 'EastEnders'. MICHELLE sinks to the floor, then plays her Patsy Cline record, quietly.*

RACHEL: Who's this?

MICHELLE: Patsy Cline.

RACHEL: Who?

MICHELLE: Patsy Cline.

RACHEL: Patsy Cline. Never heard of her.

MICHELLE: There's a film about her.

RACHEL: What?

MICHELLE: There's a film about her. With Jessica Lange. I got it out on video. (*She moves toward RACHEL.*) She died tragically. In an aeroplane.

RACHEL: Close your eyes.

*RACHEL holds perfume under MICHELLE's nose.*

MICHELLE: Mmm.

RACHEL : Want some?

MICHELLE: Yes please.

*MICHELLE holds out wrists, ears. RACHEL dabs perfume on them. MICHELLE sits on floor next to RACHEL.*

MICHELLE: Is it teatime yet?

RACHEL: Not yet. Not hungry, are you?

MICHELLE: No. Just wondered if it was teatime. (*She listens to the record.*) This is my favourite record. Barbara hates it. She tells me to turn it down.

*RACHEL tickles MICHELLE.*

RACHEL: Turn it down. Turn it down. Turn it down. I think it's that tickling finger.

MICHELLE: Don't! Don't!

*MICHELLE tries to tickle RACHEL.*

RACHEL: You can't tickle me. I might have my baby.

*MICHELLE lays her hands on RACHEL's knee.*

RACHEL: You still got ticklish knees?

*RACHEL tickles MICHELLE.*

MICHELLE: No! No!

RACHEL: Let's put one of my records on.

*MICHELLE goes to the record rack. She picks out one, brings it back to RACHEL. RACHEL reads the label.*

RACHEL: The Beatles.

MICHELLE: (*Putting on the record*) Barbara likes the Beatles.

*'Twist and Shout' plays.*

## Scene Eight
## Joyous Sisterhood

*RACHEL sits, takes out a Boots bag containing three lipsticks. She takes out her lipstick and applies it.*

MICHELLE: Give me mine.

*RACHEL hands a lipstick to MICHELLE. MICHELLE puts it on. RACHEL hands her a lipstick for BARBARA. MICHELLE takes it to her.*

MICHELLE: Barbara. Barbara. Put it on. Put it on.

*BARBARA puts on the lipstick. MICHELLE and RACHEL watch over her shoulder.*

BARBARA: What do you think, Mich?

MICHELLE: It's nice.

*BARBARA kisses MICHELLE. MICHELLE traces the kiss with her hand. RACHEL kisses BARBARA. MICHELLE dances the twist.*

MICHELLE: Dance with me, Rachel.

*RACHEL declines.*

MICHELLE: Dance with me, Barbara.

*BARBARA and MICHELLE dance the twist until BARBARA stops, exhausted. MICHELLE brings a chair for her.*

MICHELLE: Sit down.

*BARBARA sits.* MICHELLE turns the record player off.

RACHEL: Mum liked the Beatles.

*MICHELLE kneels, facing BARBARA and RACHEL.*

BARBARA: And she liked (*Sings*) 'The Deadwood stage is coming over the hill...' (*etc*)

*BARBARA continues to sing the song. RACHEL joins in. BARBARA encourages MICHELLE to join in too.*

MICHELLE: Dad's (*Sings*) 'There'll be blue birds over, the white cliffs of Dover...' (*etc*)

BARBARA: Oh, Dad.

*BARBARA and RACHEL join in.*

BARBARA: Rachel's (*Sings*) 'We're all going on a, summer holiday...' (*etc*)

*RACHEL and MICHELLE join in on the line, 'We're going where the sun shines brightly...'.*

RACHEL: It didn't – it rained the whole holiday.

BARBARA: Yes – chewing gum!

RACHEL: And canvas seats!

MICHELLE: I don't remember that.

RACHEL: You were little then.

BARBARA: Mine (*Sings*) 'Memories...' (*etc*)

RACHEL: Sing us yours, Mich.

*MICHELLE stands unsteadily, faces them, and sings 'I Fall to Pieces', using her lipstick as a microphone. When she finishes, there is silence.*

BARBARA: What are we going to do, Michelle? What's going to become of us? What are we going to do for the rest of our lives? Stay home and wait for someone to call? Play Patsy Cline records over and over again? Grow old together like two dusty old birds in a cage? What kind of life is that?

## Scene Nine
## Michelle Finds her own Voice

MICHELLE: (*To RACHEL*) That's my favourite record. Barbara hates it, don't you, Barbara? She tells me to turn it down, don't you? Is it teatime yet, Rachel? Usually we buy everything low-fat – low-fat crisps, low-fat cheeses, low-fat spreads. We'll all have to go to Tesco's at Culverhouse Cross on Thursday to do 'the big shop' won't we, Rachel?

RACHEL: No, Michelle, we won't.

MICHELLE: Usually we go on Thursday afternoons to do 'the big shop'...

RACHEL: I can't live like that, Michelle.

MICHELLE: Usually we get everything low-fat – low-fat crisps, low-fat cheeses, low-fat spreads – Barbara!

103

*BARBARA rises, walks to the wall, and stands facing it.*

MICHELLE: Usually we go to the coffeeshop – usually we have a light snack...

RACHEL: I know that, I know.

*RACHEL rises.*

MICHELLE: Barbara, Barbara, Barbara.

RACHEL: Let her be.

MICHELLE: Barbara, Barbara. Usually on a Thursday afternoon...

RACHEL: Does it matter, Michelle?

MICHELLE: Usually we go to Tesco's at Culverhouse Cross on a Thursday afternoon to do 'the big shop'...

RACHEL: Does it matter what day you do the shopping?

*MICHELLE begins circling the room and continues to do so as she speaks. During her speech, BARBARA turns slowly and watches.*

| MICHELLE: | RACHEL: |
|---|---|
| My room's pale duck-blue | I can't live like this. |
| and it's got white emulsion | |
| on the doors and windows | |
| and it's got pale blue | |
| curtains | |
| and it's my room | I can't live like this. |
| and it's got dark blue carpet | I can't live like this, |

and pale duck-blue walls
and white furnishings
and a white wardrobe
and a white dressing table
and a white bedside table
and it's my room
it's my room
it's my room
it's my room
we'll all have to go to Tesco's
at Culverhouse Cross
on Thursday afternoon
Barbara Barbara Barbara
it's got my things in it –
my things
it's got a blue lampshade
and a blue bedside lamp
and an alarm clock
and a radio alarm
and in the drawer I keep my
personal things
I keep my crystal earrings
and I keep my purse
and I keep my savings bank-
book
and in my wardrobe
I keep my blouses and my
skirts
and my jumpers and my coats
and it's my room
my room
my room
mine
that's where I am me –
in my room

Michelle.
There's more to life than
'the big shop' at
Culverhouse Cross,
Michelle.

Stop hiding, Michelle.

Life's too precious

What do you want,
Michelle.
What do you really
want?

Tell me what you want
Michelle.
What do you really
want?

I don't want you to force me
to speak
I don't want you to force me
to speak.

*MICHELLE stops circling and faces the audience.*

I don't know what I want,
I don't know
I don't know what I want.

*RACHEL goes to MICHELLE. They embrace. MICHELLE
turns to look at BARBARA.*

ALL: (*Sing*) Soave s'il vento
          Tranquilla sia l'onda
          Ed ogni elemento
          Benigno risponda
          Al nostri desir

          Soave s'il vento
          Tranquilla sia l'onda
          Ed ogni elemento
          Benigno risponda
          Al nostri desir
          Al nostri desir

BARBARA: (*Sing*)        RACHEL/MICHELLE: (*Sing*)
Benigno risponda       Al nostri desir
                     Benigno risponda
                     Al nostri desir

ALL: (*Sing*) Al nostri desir
          Al nostri desir
          Al nostri desir
          Al nostri desir....

*Provisional ending.*

*MICHELLE touches BARBARA's hand, then takes the record off and puts it back in the rack. RACHEL sits, and takes an apple from the rucksack.*

RACHEL: Barbara, want some? Michelle, want some?

MICHELLE: Yes, please.

*BARBARA takes a knife and plate from the box, and gives them to RACHEL. RACHEL cuts the apple into three, and offers a piece to BARBARA, then MICHELLE. They both take a piece.*

MICHELLE: I'm going to put my poster up.

*MICHELLE uses BluTac and ladder to put up her poster, then sits.*

*BARBARA puts the rug back on the floor, then takes out her magazine. She plays her Brahms record, then lies on the rug, reading her magazine.*

*RACHEL unpacks her diary, and reads.*

*HOUSE LIGHTS down.*

The cast of *Wishful Thinking*, February 1990

# Talking to Wordsworth

# Gillian Clarke

First performed at the Sherman Studio Theatre, Cardiff, and broadcast live by BBC Radio Wales, 1 March 1997.

## Cast:

| | | |
|---|---|---|
| Nurse Evans | – | Erica Eirian |
| Lil | – | Menna Trussler |
| Arthur | – | Glyn Houston |
| Poet | – | Sharon Morgan |

All other characters played by the cast.

## Creative Team:

| | | |
|---|---|---|
| Director | – | Phil Clark |
| Producer | – | Alison Hindell |

A co-production by BBC Radio Wales Drama and the Sherman Theatre Company.

## Poems:

| | | |
|---|---|---|
| 'O what can you give me' from *Gwalia Deserta* | – | Idris Davies |
| 'I was born in Rhymney' | – | Idris Davies |
| 'Break, break, break' | – | Alfred, Lord Tennyson |
| 'Ozymandias' | – | Percy B Shelley |
| 'Daffodils' | – | William Wordsworth |

*The Day Room of the Occupational Therapy department of a mental hospital, on St David's Day. There is the sound of a tea trolley, cups and saucers, chatter, and daytime television.*

NURSE EVANS: Put that television off, someone. Arthur? You're near it, my love.

*The sound of the the television stops. Other sounds continue.*

NURSE EVANS: Come on everybody, our visitor's coming any minute. We've got to have this place tidy or what'll she think of us.

LIL: Gasping for air by the window. An' reading 'is book. That's all 'e thinks about.

NURSE EVANS: Come on Lil. Help with the tea. And leave him be. Leave Arthur alone!

LIL: She's ere! She's got a red car. She don't look like a poet. She's got a trouser suit on.

PATIENTS: (*Rush to look, call out*) Here she is.

NURSE EVANS: Come in. We have been looking forward to meeting you, haven't we ladies and gentlemen?

PATIENTS: (*In chorus*) Yes.

NURSE EVANS: Come and have a cup of tea and meet the patients. Can I take your coat?

LIL: Specially Arthur. 'Im over by the window. 'E loves poetry. 'E's got a book of it. 'E don't speak.

111

NURSE EVANS: Give her a chance, Lil. She's only just arrived.

LIL: 'E likes bluebells. 'E's got a picture of bluebells. Lovely it is. In a wood. 'Is social worker says it's from 'is 'ouse. When 'e was a kid. Are you a poetess? You famous then? D'you want my autograph? (*She cackles with laughter.*)

NURSE EVANS: Come on everyone. One cake each. AND a plate, please, Bert. We don't want crumbs do we. There's the sugar. Milk by there.

NURSE EVANS: Lil, I won't tell you again. Leave our visitor to have her tea. You can come and chat later when we're ready. (*To POET*) Good journey? Found your way all right?

POET: Fine, thanks. Beautiful coming up the valley.

NURSE EVANS: Yes, it's a lovely place. It all helps with the patients. (*To ARTHUR*) Shut that window, Arthur! We'll all catch our death.

*Sash window closes.*

POET: What are the problems? They don't look ill exactly.

NURSE EVANS: Thank you Lil. Five minutes peace please. (*To POET*) I can't discuss the patients of course. But everything. Depression. Autism. Schizophrenia. Alzheimer's. Amnesia. Learning difficulties. Some are so institutionalised, so-called Care in the Community is too late for them.... (*To LIL*) GO AWAY, LIL! You know what they say about eavesdroppers. (*To POET*) Arthur – he's an old miner – an elected mute. Intelligent man, mind. He's got dust, too. No one comes to see him. His family don't want to know. Most of the old ones are alone in the world. It's a treat for them to have someone come in from outside. Something different.

POET: He can't speak?

NURSE EVANS: Never said a word since he's been here. Depression it is, really. Nothing wrong with his vocal cords. It's in his mind. Mute.

POET: God, that would kill me! You know what they say. Gift of the gab. Kissing the blarney stone. Can't anything be done for him?

LIL: Nothing can't be done. Nothing. Nothing. Nothing.

PATIENT: Nothing on the telly.

PATIENT: Nothing in my cup neither.

PATIENT: Nurse! Dai's 'ad two slices an I 'aven't 'ad nothing.

NURSE EVANS: Wait your turn. Dai! That's enough. What will our visitor think? Dai, I'm not telling you again or you go out. Do as Nurse Jones says. Make him wait till last, Nurse Jones.

PATIENT: I'm 'aving yours, Dai.

*Laughter and catcalls from the PATIENTS.*

NURSE EVANS: We do our best. Some say singing can help with the speech but it can't cure the mind. We put

*Songs of Praise* on for them, and the Welsh one. Lil likes that. They sing along. But Arthur just reads his book, or looks out of the window. Excuse me a moment. (*To ARTHUR*) ARTHUR! CLOSE IT NOW.

*Sash window slams shut.*

ARTHUR: (*Silently*) 'O what can you give me?
Say the sad bells of Rhymney.
Is there hope for the future?
Cry the brown bells of Merthyr.'

NURSE EVANS: There's a good boy, Arthur.

LIL: Cat's got 'is tongue.

NURSE EVANS: Mind your own business, Lil.

POET: Mute! Like you hush a 'cello by putting your hand on the strings. What about the others?

NURSE EVANS: Some very intelligent people here. They're the quiet ones. Mental illness is no respecter of persons. We've got all sorts. Bank manager. Solicitor. Secretaries. Housewives. The lady in the corner – Mair – she's 96. Old head teacher. She's blind now, and quite deaf. She likes the radio. Something highbrow, like *Woman's Hour*. We got her some headphones.

POET: We could bring her to the front for the reading. It must be awful to have a lively mind trapped in an old body.

NURSE EVANS: No. They're like children. They all have their chairs. She won't move from there. She's very stubborn.

114

POET: She's got such an intelligent face.

NURSE EVANS: And Arthur refuses to budge from the window. If I turn my back he's got it open, winter or summer, and they're all grumbling about the draught. He loves being in a draught. Never mind the weather.

POET: Bird in a cage. A big, handsome man like that shut inside himself. What about the library? Does he get books?

NURSE EVANS: Oh, he's got a book. They're obsessive. They don't like change.

ARTHUR: (*Silently*) 'I was born in Rhymney
     To a miner and his wife.
     On a January morning
     I was pulled into this life.'

LIL: 'E's down the pit, that's where 'e is. Breathin' air from the down-draft. The shaft come up in the woods. They pumps it round. My Emlyn says at snap-time if the wind's right you can smell an orange half a mile away the minute a man puts 'is teeth into it. In the spring you can smell bluebells down there. Honest to God you can. And rain.

PATIENT: It's raining, it's pouring
      The old man is snoring.

LIL: 'E's the snorer. 'E'd wake the devil, 'e would.

NURSE EVANS: Lil! What did I say? Stop stirring. Give out the daffodils and leeks.

LIL: Who do want a daffodil and who do want a leek? What are you 'avin' Bert? There you go, Bert. Arthur darling? Im-o-gen?

PATIENT: Thanks Lil.

PATIENT: Nurse Jones, I haven't got a pin.

PATIENT: This one's broke. I want a new one.

NURSE EVANS: Don't put it in your tea, Bert. It'll die. And you'll be ill.

LIL: If you want a bit of coal, come to Lil. Number six. I always got a bit over. There's only me now. They've all gone. All my boys. 'E 'ad dust. Coughed up black and went. My boys are up in London. They got good jobs so they don't need no coal.

NURSE EVANS: Lil, go away now. Leave our visitor in peace. She doesn't want to be bothered with you while she's having her tea. Go on. Daffodils for ladies. Leeks for gentlemen. More by there in the jug.

POET: Thank you, Lil, I'd love a daffodil.

NURSE EVANS: A real cloth-ears is Lil. You have to be firm with her. Cruel to be kind. I'm sorry about her behaviour. One of her manic days. Other times she does nothing but sulk. I don't know which is worse. Don't believe a word she tells you. (*She claps her hands loudly.*) Right now, ladies and gentlemen. Let's get on with our tea then I can introduce our visitor. Settle down a minute. I'm talking to you. Arthur! Shut that window!

*The noise continues – chat and clattering cups.*

NURSE EVANS: Not in here, darling. It's not very nice. Harold, leave her be.

*An outbreak of fuss from the PATIENTS.*

NURSE EVANS: Oh my God, what's happened now?

*Bird sounds – tweeting and fluttering in the room.*

POET: Oh, look! It's flown in through the window!

*LIL screams and drops the jug. Shrieks and laughter from the PATIENTS. LIL is hysterical.*

NURSE EVANS: That's Arthur again. Look at that window.

LIL: Oh my God! My nerves is bad. I got a phobia about feathers. A bird in the 'ouse! It'll peck someone's eyes out. It's bad luck! Get it out of 'ere. It's done a poop on the sofa. It's an omen, thas what it is. Someone's goin' to die. Get it out!

POET: No, Lil, it's not unlucky. It's beautiful. It's just a little blue tit. Look at the colour! Poor thing. It's more scared than you are. Come on, stay by me. It's all right. It's all right.

NURSE EVANS: Everyone sit down. Stand still or sit down just where you are. Nobody move. Nurse Jones, fetch the mop. And the dustpan. I don't want anyone cutting themselves. Lil, it's all right my love. Do shut up now. Arthur, what are you doing?

117

LIL: Arthur! It'll peck your eyes out. Down came a black-bird and pecked off 'er...

POET: Look! He's got it. Arthur's caught it. Look at that! Wonderful! He's made a cage with his fingers. Little bird safe in Arthur's big hands. There it goes! Flying free in the sky.

NURSE EVANS: Well done, Arthur. (*To LIL*) You can come out from under there now, Lil. (*To ARTHUR*) Now shut the window.

*The window closes with a bang. LIL whimpers, melodramatically.*

LIL: Oh my god. It could 'ave pecked my eyes out.

NURSE EVANS: Nonsense, Lil. Come and sit by here. (*She claps her hands for silence.*)

PATIENTS: Sh! Sh! Sh!

NURSE EVANS: Right! That little problem's over. Sit down all of you and don't slip on the wet lino. Today we are lucky to have a very special guest. A poet! (*To POET*) Should I call you poetess? No? There you are. (*To PATIENTS*) A real live poet. (*To POET*) Oh! Have you published any books? You have! (*To PATIENTS*) A real live published poet. And when we've finished our tea she is going to read some poetry to us. I hope you are going to give our visitor a warm welcome.

PATIENT: Boring!

*Small outburst of male laughter.*

NURSE EVANS: That's enough, Wayne, or you'll go out. (*To POET*) He doesn't mean it. Take no notice.

*Sound of applause, murmurs, cups, coughs, chairs scraping, PATIENTS preparing to settle and calling each other.*

MALE PATIENT: Sit by me, darling! We'll have a cwtsh in the back row!

FEMALE PATIENT: You're a dirty devil, Tudor Rees. I'm telling my 'usband on you.

LIL: Coughed up black. 'E never complained. "Don't do to complain, Lil," 'e said. It's quiet in the 'ouse now. My boys come down regular from London to see their mam. They'll be in 'ere now any minute to drive me away in the Rolls.

NURSE EVANS: Yes, yes! Sit down Lil. (*To POET*) You have to laugh or you'd go mad.

POET: I nearly said, "It's a madhouse!" I'll watch my language in future. It's so easy to say the wrong thing. We don't think, do we?

NURSE EVANS: Don't worry about it. We all do it. The patients don't mind. That's how they talk themselves. It's the word-police that get me. They don't have to watch the patients as well as their tongues.

POET: But language is so powerful. It makes us what we are. I don't want to hurt people with words.

NURSE EVANS: Political correctness! It's rubbish if you ask me. Sticks and stones can break your bones...

POET: But words can hurt you. You never forget a sarcastic teacher.

NURSE EVANS: True, if you put it like that. Look at that Arthur now. Wouldn't hurt him for the world. (*To ARTHUR*) You all right, Arthur my love?

ARTHUR: (*Silently*) 'And there were strikes and lock-outs
     And meetings in the Square,
     When Cook and Smith and Bevan
     Electrified the air.'

LIL: Arthur. D'you want a leek or a daffodil, cariad? There you are then, lovely boy. You 'ave a daffodil. I'll 'ave your leek and make some cawl with it tonight. Come down my 'ouse and 'ave a dish of cawl with Lil.

NURSE EVANS: You and your cawl, Lil. Go on now. Give one to Mair.

LIL: Mair. Cheer up and 'ave a daffodil.

ARTHUR: (*Silently*) 'And I walked my native hillsides
     In sunshine and in rain,
     And learnt the poet's language
     To ease me of my pain.'

NURSE EVANS: He's off with the fairies most of the time.

LIL: Between you and me most of them is mental.

NURSE EVANS: Lil!

ARTHUR: (*Silently*) 'With Wordsworth and with Shelley
     I scribbled out my dreams

> Sometimes among the slag-heaps
> Sometimes by mountain streams.'

NURSE EVANS: Sometimes you can see he's listening. He's deep, I'll say that for him. I dare say he'd surprise us all if he could speak.

LIL: Not all there! 'E reads, mind. 'E's got books. One's called 'The Golden Treasury'. I likes that. Sounds like a shop in Cardiff. We went on a trip an' the shops 'ad names like that. They didn't 'ave Manchester House, Draper and Haberdasher, or E Jones Family Butcher. They all got names like books now.

NURSE EVANS: Lil!

POET: No, leave her. I can see a bit of myself in Lil. I like her talking. Better than poetry to hear her. Go on, Lil, I'm listening.

LIL: The nurse 'ad to read 'em to me cause I 'aven't got no glasses. I can read, only I 'aven't got no glasses. They stole 'em off me.

NURSE EVANS: Don't believe a word of it.

LIL: 'The Golden Treasury'! It's a leather book with gold writing. We 'ad some like that, a whole row of them. Encyclopaedias. Like in the miners' library. Emlyn got them for the boys. From a man at the door. Nothing like education, Emlyn said. An' 'e was right. They were big readers, my boys. They got jobs in London now.

POET: Do you like books, Lil? What's your favourite book?

LIL: 'Aven't got no glasses. They stole my glasses. But we 'ad the Encyclopaedia. All gold and brown. The doctors stole my glasses.

NURSE EVANS: Yes, yes, Lil, and I'm Ryan Giggs. (*To POET*) Hyperactive. She'd talk the hind legs off a donkey. Just wants attention. Doesn't do to encourage her. When she's depressed she goes all quiet. Got to watch her all the time.

POET: She's a bit of a poet too.

*NURSE EVANS claps for quiet.*

NURSE EVANS: Give us a minute to clear the tea things, then I'll settle them down and we can begin. We don't often have someone in to talk to them. Enough trouble shutting Lil up and the quiet ones keep themselves to themselves. It's Nurse Jones' idea. Some of them don't take to the basket-making. Art is good though. They all have a go at that.

ARTHUR: (*Silently*) 'And in this time of tumult
                 I can only hope and cry
                 That season will follow season
                 And beauty shall not die.'

LIL: Arthur's got a lot of words in 'is 'ead. 'E must 'ave, with all that reading. Something's broke between 'is brain and 'is tongue. 'Is soul 'ave gone. Snapped like a string. Cat 'ad 'is tongue, we say. Arthur! There's a lady come to read poetry to us! You'll like that my darling! You 'ave to shout at 'im. They always shouts at the twp ones. 'E's in a world of 'is own. Like 'e's listening to water. Look at 'im now! Off talking to Wordsworth.

122

ARTHUR: (*Silently*) 'Break, break, break
                On thy cold grey stones, O Sea!
                And I would that my tongue could utter
                The thoughts that arise in me.'

LIL: Fair do's, Arthur's not a snob like 'er over by there. She won't talk and there's nothing wrong with 'er tongue. Sits staring at the wall with 'er back to us. Rude, she is. Ignorant. "Thank you so much, Lil," and don't even look at me when I takes 'er tea. 'As to 'ave real china.

POET: Don't you like a pretty cup and saucer, Lil?

LIL: See Adrian over there? Lovely boy, Adrian. 'E's got shitsophrenia. Hears voices. 'E's OK today.

NURSE EVANS: Lil, where you going to sit? Have you finished giving them out?

LIL: 'Im, 'e's a teacher. Kids made 'im go off 'is 'ead. Kids these day needs a good thrashing. I'd give them one if they was one of mine. Drugs! Language! They want their bottoms smacked. If they'd 'ad the Encyclopaedia they'd be too busy workin' and rubbin' their sore bums to 'ave time for evil. (Of ARTHUR) Look at 'im now! 'E's got that funny look.

ARTHUR: (*Silently*) '...near them on the sand
      Half sunk, a shattered visage lies, whose frown
      And wrinkled lip, and sneer of cold command,
      Tell that its sculptor well those passions read
      Which yet survive, stamped on these lifeless things,
      The hand that mocked them, and the heart that fed.'

POET: Deep waters. Who shall sound that deep? What goes on in that mute, handsome, old head of yours, Arthur? And the other silent ones? Poor Mair. And Imogen with that absent look. She looks like the loyal secretary to an autocrat. Married to a bully, I bet.

NURSE EVANS: Everyone come and sit down in these chairs now. Down the front if you want to hear. Bert! That's enough, darling! Imogen! Do join us, dear. Mair, you come too. We'll help you, my dear. Come on, Pauline. Gladys. Megan. Dai. Down the front, Mair, you'll enjoy this, love. Come on, you've all got to be good today.

*A commotion of movement and fuss.*

LIL: Got to be good! Them nurses! Mrs Jenkins, if you don't mind. And Bopa Lil when I says and not before. A bloody cheek if you ask me. 'Er-in-the-corner – Imogen, there's a name! – she won' even look. For once I don' blame 'er.

NURSE EVANS: Imogen, down here, please. This is specially for you. And you, Arthur! Put your book away and come by here. Come on my darling, you love poetry. And close that window!

*The window is closed.*

ARTHUR: (*Silently*) 'And on the pedestal
    these words appear:
    "My name is Ozymandias, king of kings;
    Look on my works ye Mighty, and despair."'

*Sound of PATIENTS moving chairs, and calling to eath other.*

NURSE EVANS: Now half of them are off to the toilet. Worse than kids. You'd better keep it short, if you don't mind. They haven't a lot of concentration. They're not used to people talking to them. Can't keep their minds on words.

ARTHUR: (*Silently*) 'Nothing beside remains.
  Round the decay
    Of that colossal wreck, boundless and bare
    The lone and level sands stretch far away.'

POET: Of course. Don't worry. I'll play it by ear.

LIL: Don't take no notice. I'm sick of bloody baskets. You goin' to sing to us too? I do love words, especially when they got tunes. Can you sing 'The Green Green Grass of Home?'

POET: I'm not much of a singer. But I agree with you, Lil. Words are great. Poems are songs, really. Rhythm and tune. We all like a bit of "Oo! Ah! Can-to-na!"

LIL: Oo! Ah! Can-to-na! Oo! Ah! Can-to-na! (*Laughs raucously.*)

LIL: We 'as painting Tuesday. We done daffodils this week. I likes copying. The teacher don' like it but I gets a postcard and I copies it. 'E'd rather us make a 'orrible mess. "Expressin ourselves" 'e calls it. But I likes to be tidy. I sweeps this floor ten times a day. Nine, and I can't get to sleep for worryin' about it.

NURSE EVANS: No. Bert. You've been already. Nurse Jones, can you get them to come in now?

LIL: The art teacher says, "Well paint me a nice tidy room then, Lil, like..." whatisname. My favourite painter. Dutch, 'e is I think. 'E does lovely clean rooms with squared lino.

POET: Vermeer. Is that the one? He's my favourite too.

LIL: That's 'im! "Use your brush to SWEEP the paper." You got to laugh. 'E's nice though. We done daffodils for St David's Day.

POET: So I see. The room looks lovely, just like a garden.

LIL: Ooh! You can tell you're a poet. You says lovely things. We're 'aving an Eis-tedd-fod! 'Er-in-the-corner won't sing. An' Arthur'll just stare at 'is book. Not a word from 'im. 'E 'asn't got no words. They're locked up in that book of 'is.

ARTHUR: (*Silently*) 'I wandered lonely as a cloud...'

NURSE EVANS: Not in here, please, Bert! Manners, if you don't mind. I won't tell you again. At last. We're all here. ready to begin. What a song and dance!

LIL: I can sing. "You got a lovely little voice Lil," Emlyn says.

NURSE EVANS: Lil, that's enough or you go out.

LIL: (*Petulantly*) She's always pickin' on me. I'm tellin' the doctor on you.

ARTHUR: (*Silently*) 'Ten thousand saw I at one glance...'

LIL: 'E's got a cloud on 'is mind, the doctor says. 'E can't speak.

NURSE EVANS: Lil!

ARTHUR: (*Silently*) '...lonely as a cloud
    That floats on high o'er vales and hills...'

POET: It's lovely to be with you on this special day, and there's no better way to celebrate than with poetry. I'm sure some of us were put off poetry at school, and that's a pity because poetry's as natural as song and dance. We all like rhythm and rhyme...

ARTHUR: (*Silently*) 'When all at once I saw a crowd
        A host of golden daffodils...'

POET: And there is one special poem I'd like to start with today.

LIL: Did you write it for us then?

POET: I'll be reading one of mine in a minute, Lil, but I'd like to start with a few poems by famous poets I'm sure we all learned at school when we were children. Does anyone know a poem by heart?

PATIENT: The Boy Stood on the Burning Deck!

PATIENT: There was a young lady from Splott!

PATIENT: Yeah! Tha's a rude one. You got any rude ones Miss?

NURSE EVANS: That's enough. You're not down the rugby club now. Come and sit by me, Wayne. Right. Settle down. Settle down. Take no notice, Imogen.

*Sound of PATIENTS calling out, murmuring. A chair scraped across the floor. ARTHUR stands up. The PATIENTS are quiet, for a moment.*

NURSE EVANS: Arthur, sit down. Nurse Jones, sit by Arthur. I don't want them getting excited.

ARTHUR: (*In a cracked, robotic monotone*) I... I... I...

NURSE EVANS: Nurse Jones, stay by him.

POET: Go on, Arthur, I'm listening.

LIL: Arthur! 'As your soul come back?

*PATIENTS continue to murmur.*

ARTHUR: (*In a strained voice, as if his voicebox were artificial*) I... I... I... always liked the Romantics.

NURSE EVANS: Arthur?

NURSE JONES: Shall I call the doctor?

POET: No! Wait! Listen to him! Please. Go on, Arthur.

ARTHUR: (*His voice gathering strength*) I... I... I... wandered... lonely... as a cloud... (*In a normal voice*)
    'I wandered lonely as a cloud
    That floats on high o'er vales and hills,
    When all at once I saw a crowd,
    A host of golden daffodils.'

LIL: Arthur's got 'is tongue back!

NURSE EVANS: I've never known him do this before. Perhaps he's getting a bit over-excited. Fetch his medicine, Nurse Jones.

POET: No! It's a poem. Arthur, I'm listening to you.

*As ARTHUR speaks, the room falls silent.*

ARTHUR: 'When all at once I saw a crowd
> A host of golden daffodils:
> Beside the lake, beneath the trees,
> Fluttering and dancing in the breeze.
> Continuous as the stars that shine
> And twinkle on the milky way,
> They stretched in never-ending line
> Along the margin of the bay:
> Ten thousand saw I at one glance,
> Tossing their heads in sprightly dance.

The waves beside them danced, but they
Out-did the sparkling waves in glee:
A poet could not but be gay,
In such a jocund company;
I gazed- and gazed- but little thought
What wealth the show to me had brought:

For oft, when on my couch I lie
In vacant or in pensive mood,
They flash upon that inward eye
Which is the bliss of solitude;
And then my heart with pleasure fills,
And dances with the daffodils.'

*Inside: silence. Outside the window: a song-thrush sings.*

# The Gate

**Charles Way**

First broadcast in full by BBC Radio Wales,
2 January 2000.


Cast:


Bryn – Andrew Rivers
Father – Owen Garmon
Sally – Manon Edwards
Mother

All other characters played by the cast.


Creative Team:

Director – Jeremy Grainger
Producer


A play for voices written for BBC Radio Wales. This is an edited version that can be performed script-in-hand.

*The PEOPLE OF THE TOWN are the voices that swirl, dream-like, around BRYN. They change roles continually, from the local choir, to the customers of a busy pub, to schoolkids rushing home. All the speaking characters can emerge from this group.*

BRYN: (*To audience*) I'm walking up to a certain gate where my late father used to catch a breather. The summit is five hundred feet above, wearing a shawl of thin cloud. As kids, the gate marked a welcome stop; a seat from which to mock the ground achieved, and gather strength for the final push. In the early days he'd always reach the gate first and watch our breathless progress up the slope, grinning as we collapsed, all lungs and legs. (*He arrives, opens the gate.*) The gate in question is nothing grand – a tidy gate that separates the upland from the lowland, the bracken from the grass, the earth from the heavens. Its five bars give two opposing views: the hills behind, the plains beyond, and of course the town below. My father liked this place, this view. I'm always aware of his presence here; his ghost leaning on the gate, forever on the moorland side, looking down with wary eyes over the scene of his life and his untimely death.

*The sound of the wind blowing across the moorland.*

BRYN: (*To audience*) I remember reading once in school, how Odysseus talked to his old friend Achilles in the Halls of the Dead, a cup of blood gave the hero voice. I only have a flask of tea, and a drop of brandy hidden in my haversack – to bring him my Father back. I drink a toast to his memory, and then out of the moving mist I see his familiar stoop.

*The sound of breath.*

133

BRYN: (*To audience*) Suddenly he's here, complete with walking gear, the same stick, the same sigh on arrival. I offer him the silver flask – that once was his. The brandy blood runs down his soul, warms his dry tongue. 'How are you son,' he says. 'I'm doing well,' I lie.

FATHER: How is your mother?

BRYN: Bit lonely.

FATHER: To be expected.

BRYN: (*To audience*) There I go, accusing him, laying on the guilt with the family trowel, as if his death was the death he wanted. But it's too early yet to push the gate wide open. Best circumnavigate the globe, as families often do, before going down that road.

FATHER: How's the town shaping up?

BRYN: They want to move the cattle market.

FATHER: Move it? Where?

BRYN: Out of town.

FATHER: What for?

BRYN: The slaughter house needs to be modernised. Lorries need better access.

FATHER: Ach, development.

BRYN: It's real estate.

134

FATHER: It won't be a market town without a market, will it? And what's that down there? That mark across the plain?

BRYN: That's the new road, the one you said would only bring good things to the town.

FATHER: Well, it's a fine road I can see that. Makes it easy for folk to come and go. A man could leave and be beyond the reach of all he knows before he had time to think.

BRYN: (*To audience*) He has seen right through me as if I were the ghost at hand.

FATHER: Are you leaving then?

BRYN: Thinking about it. That's why I'm up here sitting on the gate, surveying the scene, weighing up the options.

FATHER: Where would you go?

BRYN: I don't know.

FATHER: Another town?

BRYN: It's just a place, Dad, nothing special. I never meant to stop here.

FATHER: No one ever does, I never did. All the same, it's a good town – a place to be and belong. And the point is, it's small enough to actually exist. (*He remains on the gate throughout the whole play.*)

*Enter the PEOPLE OF THE TOWN, as the local church choir, singing a plain chant.*

135

BRYN: (*To audience*) It's small alright. From this distance I can lay the entire construct in the palm of my hand and swallow it whole. A little big town on the banks of a slow river. Town of my first breath, town of my first kiss, someone else's breath. Town of love lost and found and lost again.

VICAR: We will meet again next Tuesday, God willing, at 7.30pm. 7.30 sharp.... (*To BRYN*) Bryn, how nice to see you.

BRYN: Thank you, Vicar.

VICAR: Excuse the mess – the choir, the deadly choir. Are you well?

BRYN: Yes. Just came here for a think, you know.

VICAR: I see, I see.

BRYN: (*To audience*) He nods, head to one side, his mind skipping back through a catalogue of christenings and weddings, until he reaches my divorce.

VICAR: I had a chat to... to... to Sally.

BRYN: She said she'd been.

VICAR: So, what are your plans for the future?

BRYN: I was thinking... of trying someplace... trying somewhere... making a fresh start.

VICAR: You mean, 'leave the town'?

BRYN: (*To audience*) There's a small earthquake in his voice as if leaving was akin to mutiny, a turning back at St. Peter's gate for the sake of an unknown view.

VICAR: For what its worth, I still believe there is a way for you and Sally, after twenty years of good marriage, to be reconciled. I mean to say, that divorce is not necessarily the end. Indeed, I married a couple the other week whom I first married twenty years ago.

BRYN: She's found someone else.

VICAR: I see, I see. And your... your own ladyfriend?

BRYN: (*To audience*) There's no sense of judgement in his voice, but the sound of 'ladyfriend' hangs in the stillness of the church. For an unreasonable amount of time. (*To VICAR*) No, she... we're not together – anymore.

VICAR: I see, I see.

BRYN: (*To audience*) He stares up at what he sees, high in the church rafters which, he notes, need repairing.

VICAR: It's very good to see you, Bryn, very good indeed. And anytime you wish to... to, to... talk, please, um, though, ah, I have to show these visitors the tombs, and and do a little brass-rubbing – very keen.

BRYN: (*To audience*) Then he goes – a good man and a happy one. When he leaves he takes his country with him. But I can't believe as he believes, belong to his belonging. How lucky he is to have opened the gate and found a generous place....

*Vision of SALLY, getting ready for church.*

BRYN: (*To audience*) Unlike she – she, the woman I once loved. The woman who became my private church has not been here since we were married – apart from my father's funeral. The whole town turned up for that. Their attendance a mark of defiance – a statement, not of grief, but of belief in the beleaguered notion of the town itself. She came then in a thin, black dress. On her previous visit she wore white, of course. How simple it is to colour in our lives, it makes such perfect sense....

*Sound of wedding bells. The PEOPLE OF THE TOWN become wedding guests.*

BRYN: (*To audience*) Strange, the way a small crowd gathers outside the gates to watch a wedding, as if slowing down to stare at an accident.

*The VICAR is present, SALLY holds his arm. Confetti is thrown. The sound of bells.*

BRYN: (*To audience*) Our marriage, being as it was between two youngsters made and raised by the town, became the collective hope of the town. A photograph of you-bride, me-groom, inside the lychgate as it rained, became front-page news. We were laughing.
 Perhaps, like the town, we got to know each other too well. There's no street unknown to us, no corner of surprise. Every inch a memory, an incident – the bus stop, where I got beaten up by a future member of the Welsh Assembly; the wall, from which I slipped and cut my chin leaving a scar which gave the girls their opening line...

GIRL: Where'd you get that good-looking scar then?

BRYN: Skiing down the Matterhorn.

GIRL: You never.

BRYN: (*To audience*) The cinema, now a snooker hall, where I sat gobsmacked with Gran, as Omar Sharif rode out of the heat on a horse with humps....My first leaving was long ago, in the skull of a boy who thought he was Lawrence of Arabia skipping down the spine of a train in a dressing gown.

*SALLY approaches, cutting off BRYN's reverie.*

SALLY: Is it true?

BRYN: Is what true? (*Pause.*) Yes, it's true.

SALLY: Get out! Get out – I don't want to see you, not now, not ever.

BRYN: Never?

*SALLY becomes one of the PEOPLE OF THE TOWN agian. BRYN moves back towards his FATHER.*

FATHER: I take it things are not as they once were, between you and she.

BRYN: I don't want to think about it.

FATHER: You have to – think about it. There are children involved.

BRYN: She has found someone else....

FATHER: Best move forward then. But you don't have to leave – this is your town, your nation.

BRYN: Don't tell me, my destiny?

FATHER: Funny how they built that road alongside the railway line – like a shadow. That road changes everything. The way one arrives and leaves a place sticks in the memory. People come and go too easily. They don't face up to things.

BRYN: Meaning?

FATHER: You have your mother to think on. Now I'm gone she needs you more than ever.

BRYN: I see her every Wednesday. Every Wednesday we have a roast.

FATHER: How is she coping?

BRYN: She's moving on. Her hands have stopped shaking.

FATHER: What happened to those boys?

BRYN: They're doing time.

FATHER: Are they indeed.

BRYN: They'll be out soon.

FATHER: And that worries you?

BRYN: (*To audience*) Of course it worries me. They took you out of the warm world, put you there on the other side of the gate....

*Night sounds. TWO YOUNG MEN enter.*

BRYN: (*To audience*) My Mother heard a noise.

*Sound of breaking glass.*

BRYN: (*To audience*) Then another.

FATHER: What? What?

MOTHER: I heard a noise.

FATHER: Cats.

*Sound of a foot treading on glass.*

FATHER: I'll go.

MOTHER: No, don't go – phone the police.

FATHER: Phone's downstairs.

MOTHER: Just lock the door.

FATHER: This is my house. (*Calling out*) Who's there? What the bloody hell are you doing here?

*The TWO YOUNG MEN attack the FATHER. He falls.*

BRYN: (*To audience*) They hit him. They hit him when he was down. Two young men-lads. He'd known them all their lives; mended their bikes, ruffled their hair, had them round at Halloween. Then they became seventeen and needed cash. Not much – enough for a night's trip beyond the gate, of knowing who they were.

They lived two doors down, knew the lie of the land. Besides, the old man would be asleep. But there he was, standing in front of them in his frayed dressing-gown. And he knew them. And they smacked him over the head because he knew them, and shame swam into their hearts so they kicked him and he fell on the cold kitchen tiles. His wife upstairs frozen with fear, feeling the warmth of his body fade on the sheets....

*Sound of prison doors closing.*

BRYN: (*To audience*) He ruffled their hair. Now they're coming out, those boys with small-town grins. They'll be on the street, in the pubs, and I'll see them and they'll see me – the men who killed my father in his own good town. A place to be and belong?

*Enter MOTHER. The sound of plates and Sunday roast.*

MOTHER: Your sister called.

BRYN: How is she then?

MOTHER: She wants to come home. Had enough of London.

BRYN: She's been saying that for years. Still, it would be good – for you, I mean.

MOTHER: She can't go turning her life upside-down for me. Long as you're here, I'm alright.

BRYN: (*To audience*) She pinches my cheek between forefinger and thumb. After Dad was killed, her world reduced itself to this small space between sink and stove.

MOTHER: I don't know how anyone can live in a city.

BRYN: (*To audience*) In Mother's eyes, the wall that circled once the town never quite came down. She never quite belonged and father's family never quite forgave her. She came from off – off can be as far as Africa though in her case it was just the other side of Hereford – and they were naturally suspicious of anyone who went to church in a Cathedral.

MOTHER: Is the lamb alright?

BRYN: Lovely. Edwards?

MOTHER: Of course. I had a letter off the county – said the boys who killed your father are coming out of prison – for 'good behaviour'.

BRYN: I know.

MOTHER: I don't want you doing nothing.

BRYN: What could I do?

MOTHER: Nothing. It's time you got your life sorted out.

BRYN: Yes, I'm...

MOTHER: You tell that wife of yours...

BRYN: Sally...

MOTHER: To get on home.

BRYN: She's not coming home, Mum.

MOTHER: Nonsense. You get married – you stay together no matter what. That's the whole point of it.

BRYN: Times have changed.

MOTHER: Oh, have they indeed? And I suppose you take me for one of those old fools who say nothing else but how good things 'used' to be. Well I'm not. But I do know one thing: those boys who hit your father wouldn't have been those boys, not years ago – it wouldn't have happened, not like that, not here.

BRYN: (*To audience*) What can I say, except perhaps she's right. My town is not one to which I necessarily wish to belong. I'd rather belong to the old brown town they sell in books of yesteryear.

MOTHER: Oh I meant to say, I found a picture of your father.

BRYN: (*To audience*) This takes me unawares. Since his murder, she has kept him locked away. She even took his photo from the mantelpiece. Then she sat for a year, immured in grief, staring at the space he once occupied. Friends of Dad would call and sit with her. Old men, from his rugger-playing days; men from the Masonic lodge; men from the Con club, the Legion, the Rotary, and finally his sisters came, and the small town offered up its good heart and held her close. Now, at last, she belongs.

MOTHER: An army photo. Very smart he looks.

BRYN: You keep it, Mum.

MOTHER: No, I'd like you to have it.

BRYN: (*To audience*) The picture in my hand was taken in Poona. A dusty training camp. My father is twenty-six, wearing khaki shorts and an oversized bush hat. He became a captain, losing with gleeful rapidity the soft burr of his border tongue, replacing it with the snipped English of Kenneth More and Richard Todd. He knew how to be and how to get along.

*The sound of soft Indian music.*

BRYN: (*To audience*) He taught Sikhs and Hindus how to drive the stolid British trucks across the plains and, in return, they taught him how to wait, how to be proud and humble, at the same time. They taught him the size of the world and he would never be as happy again, in the small Marcher town of his youth.

He tried to fold up the map of his experience. He gave his accent its old job back and immersed himself in building a new empire in the town beneath the gate.

*The sound of a pub.*

FATHER: No, no – we need that road.

*The sound of men in disagreement.*

145

FATHER: No, no, this town, right, was once famous for its wool. No, wool made soft by the quality of the Usk river. That trade vanished. Why?

MAN: I think yer goin' to tell us.

*Laughter.*

MAN: I got that feeling.

*Laughter.*

FATHER: Because...

*Laughter.*

FATHER: No, no, because they built turnpike roads and the salesmen bypassed the town. Shall we be passed by again? We need that road, I'm tellin' you.

MAN: I knew you would.

*Laughter.*

FATHER: Trade needs transport, the new transport is by road. The railway is finished, over, gone.

*The PEOPLE OF THE TOWN burst into a chorus of opinion.*

BRYN: (*To audience*) He talked and he built and he became the place. Master of the Lodge, Justice of the Peace, Mayor of the well lit streets.

*The sounds of the jungle.*

BRYN: (*To audience*) But the green deepness of the jungle; the strange, erotic statues found in unnamed clearings; the wary eyes of village girls wandering home at dusk; the thin smile of a tiger caught in jeep headlights, never left his waking life.

*The sound of a steam train pulling into the station.*

BRYN: (*To audience*) The nomad in his heart had been roused. So why did he return and greet with open arms the small-town life? Are the sins of settlement so sweet?

SALLY: So, how long has it been going on?

BRYN: Not long.

SALLY: Is it over?

BRYN: Yes. (*To audience*) I lie to the mother of my children; a soon-to-be divorcee who's known me since she played Mary to my Donkey – a casting which has echoed strangely down the years.

*The PEOPLE OF THE TOWN become market traders and buyers. The sounds of market day.*

BRYN: (*To audience*) I should have learnt my lesson then: there's no escape in a two-horse town, from the misdemeanours of the flesh. When the love of your youth says enough is enough, you can't sweep out with a grand gesture, a theatrical puff, or even a shrug of 'so what?' because tomorrow you'll meet in the market hall, catch each other's eye...

SALLY: I thought this was my day.

BRYN: Yes I...

SALLY: We agreed. Tuesdays was my day.

BRYN: Yes, but... I'm...

SALLY: Sorry?

BRYN: Tuesdays is market day and has been for hundreds of years – how long do I have to stay out of town on Tuesdays?

SALLY: What?

BRYN: This agreement was temporary, I thought, regarding Tuesdays.

SALLY: You agreed; made a promise. Once again, you break it.

BRYN: I'm sorry. I told you.

SALLY: Yes.

BRYN: (*To audience*) The conversation wilts beneath the glaring heat of an ordinary life. The joyful intimacy of love that once transcended these well worn streets now reduced to half-truths and broken phrases. (*To SALLY*) I was going to have...

SALLY: No.

BRYN: A coffee.

SALLY: There's no point.

BRYN: (*To audience*) We, who believed in each other, belonged to each other, reduced ourselves for each other, glare at each other, shocked by what we have achieved. She stares right at me, as if for the last time. And then she's gone. It was her day, after all.

*The sounds of the market hall rise. Distinct VOICES can now be heard, selling and buying.*

BRYN: (*To audience*) Here, at least, relationships are simple – you give, I take; you take, I give. The rich blend of valley voice and sly country banter becomes its own plainsong...

*The sounds of vendors transform into a musical moment.*

BRYN: (*To audience*) That sings across the years. Whatever else happened to this town under the far reach of Roman rule, the terror of the Norman sword, the long siege of the English word, the people always met back here with something to sell. This is where we belong, our fingers dark with coin. Here there is rest, peace, even hope.

SELLER: Cheapest bread in town...

SELLER: Half a dozen, dear?

SELLER: Pound for a pound.

BRYN: (*To audience*) There's everything a man could want from...

SELLER: Saris...

BRYN: (*To audience*) To...

SELLER: Postcards...

BRYN: (*To audience*) To...

SELLER: Fresh fish...

BRYN: (*To audience*) And...

SELLER: Rabbits...

BRYN: (*To audience*) And religious books...

SELLER: Watches...

BRYN: (*To audience*) That live as long as butterflies...

SELLER: Homemade socks...

BRYN: (*To audience*) That will never die...

SELLER: Antique spoons...

BRYN: (*To audience*) Worn smooth by the mouths of Edwardian children. And if you've discovered too late in the day that the love of your life is actually your wife...

*The sounds of the market hall drop.*

BRYN: (*To audience*) There's a mystic from Merthyr who can ease the pain.

MYSTIC: Romance, enchantment, charms, visions, destiny, lady luck and cosmic harmony.

BRYN: I am tempted to by some...

MYSTIC: Cosmic harmony?

BRYN: No, I... I... (*To audience*) I am restricted by a chapel residue inherited from my Nan.

MYSTIC: Why don't you sit down, love. Take the weight off.

BRYN: (*To audience*) To my surprise I'm sitting down and the world fades....

MYSTIC: I uses the cards...

BRYN: (*To audience*) She says...

MYSTIC: Not to read but to point the way.

BRYN: (*To audience*) She sees that I'm troubled.

MYSTIC: I can see that yewer troubled.

BRYN: (*To audience*) That I should avoid...

MYSTIC: The colour red.

BRYN: (*To audience*) That I regretted...

MYSTIC: Things you've said.

BRYN: (*To audience*) That I might be...

MYSTIC: Moving on, before too long.

BRYN: (*To audience*) And, yes, it's curative to cry.

MYSTIC: Nothing wrong in that, love. I have cried whole seas into existence.

BRYN: (*To audience*) And she stares at me, as if my eyes were oceans too, and I retreat, shocked at my transparency.

*The full sounds of the market hall return.*

BRYN: (*To audience*) I retreat to the secondhand bookstall selling out-of-date maps and boxes of Mills & Boon. So much soul-searching, heart-wrenching love in lands far from the stone and slate of this old railway town. Perhaps the quest to be and belong, has nothing to do with country, nation, town at all?

*The PEOPLE OF THE TOWN begin to sing again, but in a moment they are singing real plainsong and thus we are transferred, once more, to the church.*

BRYN: (*To audience*) It has something to do with love. And God is something to do with love, whatever coat he wears. In this town, God has diversified, with a business acumen second to none: Baptists, Quakers, Methodists, Shakers, United and Reformed, Catholics and Salvationists, witnesses all to the fact that we – I – dare not lead an unexamined life.

*The VICAR is leading some tourists around the church.*

VICAR: This way, please. Now to... to... to the right of the altar, on the south side, is a recess in the wall, ornamented with gothic niches, is a rude figure... (*To BRYN*) Hello Bryn.

BRYN: Vicar.

VICAR: A rude figure carved in stone, of a knight, cross-legged, clad in a coat of mail. A helmet on his head, the left hand on his breast. The right hand clasping the hilt of a sword. His feet repose, as you see, on a greyhound, for some reason.

BRYN: (*To audience*) I stare at the stone figure.

VICAR: A Lord of the town who once...

BRYN: (*To audience*) Played for Wales with Llewellyn the Great.

VICAR: Beside him lies his wife...

BRYN: (*To audience*) Beside him lies... his wife. Shall we be dead one day my love and like these knights and ladies fair, lie side by side, our effigies recumbent on top a mighty sepulchre? Me, in complete armour – you know what a dab hand I was at self-defence – a motorcycle helmet on my head, my feet resting on a cricket bat. Shall I be wearing marble jeans, and that old pair of trainers you loved to hate? Perhaps you wouldn't like it, even in stone, to be forever at my side, your breasts petrified and always out of reach, except from kids who come to rub your contours and wonder what we did to earn this stony privilege, and why your nose has been forever sheared away. What was it you said?

SALLY: You are stuck here, like you have glue on your shoes.

BRYN: Ah yes, that was it: the glue on the shoes.

SALLY: You never go for what you want.

BRYN: (*To audience*) She referred, of course, to the cottage in the country. The one which symbolised our future happiness, with roses round the porch and a mortgage that lasted until the day of judgement.

*The sound of children chanting the rhyme 'Ip-dip-do, cat's got flu...' which ends on 'out goes you'.*

SALLY: So why don't you go – now. It's your chance, Bryn, to get away.

BRYN: (*To audience*) So says the Carnival Queen of 1974, who wants me now to leave the town where we grew our kids like corn, summer after summer – until this hard harvest.

*The sound of a teacher ringing a bell, and the happy sound of kids out of school.*

BRYN: Where is my boy? Hey, have you seen Owen?

KID: He's got detention, sir.

BRYN: Oh, what for?

KID: He kicked Mrs Angel.

BRYN: Oh. (*To audience*) The future runs, streams, pours round and through me. Beans from a can, fizz from a bottle, though some are slow moving, mournful, pale as a winter sky – the future can be a heavy burden – but most come out kicking, teasing, barging, tumbling, through each moment of being, aware only of the present tense.

I run through the text again. There's no way to break it gently.

(*To Owen*) Owen, I've made a choice. A voice, that keeps me up all night is telling me it's time; time to make my move, find another life, leave the ever shifting, never changing town....

OWEN: But where will you go, Dad? Can we come and see you? Don't you like the town? Don't you like us? Me? What about Rhi? You said you'd never leave. You promised! You promised me.

RHI: What are you doing here?

BRYN: Rhi?

RHI: Apart from talking to yourself?

BRYN: I wasn't.

RHI: You were. I saw your lips moving. Trying to embarrass me, or what?

BRYN: I've come to pick up Owen.

RHI: So have I. Does Mum know?

BRYN: Yes. I... I asked.

RHI: She didn't tell me.

BRYN: He's got detention – again. (*To audience*) My teenage daughter scowls at the school she once defied herself, with psychopathic gusto.

RHI: I'll go then.

BRYN: No, stay. There's something I want to, well...

RHI: What?

BRYN: Talk through.

RHI: Oh? You and Mum getting back together?

BRYN: No.

RHI: No?

BRYN: No.

RHI: What then? I got to meet Kyle.

BRYN: (*To audience*) Who is she? This daughter? Half-girl, half-woman, unsure which half she belongs to. She has rings in irretrievable places, her hair is a delicate shade of puce, and her knuckles are branded K−Y−L−E.

RHI: WHAT?

BRYN: I was thinking... of making a new start. Going some place else, somewhere new.

RHI: Why not? Go for it.

BRYN: I'm serious.

RHI: So am I. I'm leaving too. I'm not staying here – this town's a dump. I'll go to London. I could live with you. Couldn't I?

BRYN: Of course you can live with me. That's your choice.

RHI: In London?

BRYN: Wherever.

RHI: So all I have to do now like is... choose between you and Mum?

BRYN: (*To audience*) What a neat magician I turned out to be – making a childhood vanish in a single conversation. Suddenly her pale face, the dark smudge beneath her eyes, shakes my confidence. Even here I could lose her. Even in a town like this, a child can open the wrong gate and be gone. This pretty market town deceives, dissembles, with its ancient charms. Club drugs, cocaine and heroin are sold by high school kids with clear-skinned smiles....

RHI: Dad? You're doing it again.

BRYN: What?

RHI: Dreaming; staring!

BRYN: I'm just worried.

RHI: You've no need to worry about me.

BRYN: But I do.

RHI: I'm not a child anymore.

BRYN: I'm sorry, Rhi.

RHI: What for?

BRYN: For that. For all this... mess.

RHI: These things happen.

BRYN: I want you to go to college.

RHI: You don't want me to live with you in London?

BRYN: I never said I was going to London.

RHI: Perhaps I'll live with Kyle then, in Cardiff.

BRYN: Oh no, no. K−Y−L−E, who dresses only in black; writes tunes for a band called 'Deadly Text', and never washes from one suicidal song to the next.

RHI: And what about Owen?

BRYN: I wouldn't leave Owen, or you – just the town.

RHI: Just Mum, is it? And the men who killed Grandad. You'll leave them behind as well, won't you?

BRYN: (*To audience*) She is suddenly older than I have ever known.

RHI: I see them too, you know. I see them, I know them, and they know me.

BRYN: I'm sorry, Rhi.

RHI: Why? It's not your fault. You don't have to leave. Not because of them. I don't want you to leave.

BRYN: It isn't because of them.

RHI: No? So you've decided then?

BRYN: Yes. No. Yes.

RHI: (*Groans*) You sound like bloody Hamlet.

BRYN: (*To audience*) I find it sadly reassuring that she knows who Hamlet is.

RHI: I'll leave you to pick up Owen.

BRYN: Rhi?

RHI: What? (*Shouts in frustration*) What?

BRYN: I love you.

RHI: I know.

BRYN: (*To audience*) A gentle nudge of the gate and she's gone, leaving her childhood behind. A distant country that lies in wait for us all.

*The sound of the wind.*

BRYN: (*To audience*) I'm walking up to a certain gate where my late father used to catch a breather. The summit is five hundred feet above, wearing a shawl of thin cloud. As kids, the gate marked a welcome stop; a seat from which to mock the ground achieved, and gather strength for the final push. In the early days he'd always reach the gate first and watch our breathless progress up the slope, grinning as we collapsed, all lungs and legs. The gate in question is nothing grand – a tidy gate that separates the upland from the lowland, the bracken from the grass, the earth from the heavens. Its five bars give two opposing views: the hills behind, the plains beyond, and of course the town below.

My father liked this place, this view.

FATHER: So, you've made a choice.

BRYN: Yes.

FATHER: You'll stay?

BRYN: For the time being.

FATHER: For the sake of the children.

BRYN: Yes.

FATHER: And for yourself.

BRYN: Perhaps.

FATHER: Because, in the scale of things, when whole peoples are swept away by flood and war, it seems ridiculous to make yourself a refugee.

BRYN: Yes.

FATHER: Because you love the place, the line of the hills, the bend in the river, the life of the town. Because what happens here happens elsewhere – love, hate, betrayal, for-giveness, even murder. The people are the same as they always have been, shaped by the moment and their history too. As you are, as I was.

BRYN: (*To audience*) I sit on the gate and look far over town to where the Severn meets the sea. Not far above my thoughts, fighter planes scream, practising for a future war planned long ago. Beneath me, my personal history pulls

160

my vision back toward the settlement so old, so modern, and as much as any city, a fair reflection of the nation.

BRYN: Dad?

BRYN: (*To audience*) He's gone, back to the halls of the dead, leaving the gate and the town and me surveying the scene.

THE PEOPLE: The town hall, the war memorial, the bowling green, the old school, the new estate, the big house, the hospital, the supermarket, the railway cottages....

BRYN: (*To audience*) The station, from which my Grandad left for France; where Mother stepped off the train into the many lives of the always-talking town. The lychgate, where we posed for photographs on our wet wedding day.

My love, my love, everything that cannot be forgiven will be forgiven.

From here I can see a thin lane running steeply down between a line of trees, and there's a boy – freewheeling down the long slope into town, a stick of hazel strapped to the handle bars and, on the stick, bunches of daffodils – short, delicate, pale, and sixpence each. I'm yelling into the wind, now, then, forever; freewheeling, faster, faster, faster, out through the gates of time.

*The End.*

# Break
# My Heart

**Arnold Wesker**

First performed at the Sherman Theatre, Cardiff
4 June 1997.


Cast:

Maeve Lewis    –    Maxine Evans
Michael Lewis  –    Dorien Thomas


Creative Team:

Director              –    Michael Bogdanov
Designer              –    Ulrike Engelbrecht
Lighting              –    Ceri James
Producer              –    Phil Clark
Stage Manager         –    Leanne Rochefort
Deputy Stage Manager  –    Brenda Knight


Commissioned by Penderyn Films and the Sherman Theatre, Cardiff. Dedicated by the playwright to Jan Morris, for support in difficult times.

## Scene One

*An attic room in a 1930s terraced house, in any industrial Welsh town.*

*MAEVE LEWIS – short, dumpy, with a cautious vivacity, aged around thirty, worn before her time – a battered wife.*

*The attic corner is her space; her retreat. There is a desk on which sits a desktop computer, and surrounding shelves, books. She is copying from a volume into her computer the last lines of Shakespeare's 'Sonnet 147'. It's her way of learning it by heart – typing it cements it. When done, she stands away, and recites, glancing every now and then to recall a forgotten word. Her rendering is not recited but felt, as though gossiping to a neighbour, investing the sonnet with a quality of bewilderment, not understanding how love can produce such unreason, and scolding herself for her 'uncertain sickly appetite'. But, oh, how she relishes the language.*

MAEVE: (*Quoting*) My love is as a fever longing still
  For that which longer nurseth the disease,
  Feeding on that which doth preserve the ill,
  Th' uncertain sickly appetite to please.
  My reason, the physician to my love,
  Angry that his prescriptions are not kept
  Hath left me, and I desperate now approve
  Desire is death, which physic did except.
  Past cure I am, now reason is past care,
  And frantic-mad with evermore unrest,
  My thoughts and my discourse as madmen's are,
  At random from the truth vainly expressed;
  For I have sworn thee fair, and thought thee bright,
  Who art as black as hell, as dark as night.

Oh, God! And you want to write poetry, Maeve Lewis? How on earth do you dare, eh? What gives you the gall to compete with the bard?

> (*Quoting*) My love is as a fever longing still
> For that which longer nurseth the disease,
> Feeding on that which doth preserve the ill,
> Th' uncertain sickly appetite to please.

*The sound of the front door. Her husband, MICHAEL, enters. He is a joiner, and a few years older.*

MICHAEL: Maeve? Maeve? Where the fuck are you?

*MAEVE freezes – terror takes over from delight.*

MICHAEL: Up in your fucking hideaway are you? Don't you live in this fucking house any longer? Married to a fucking machine are you? I'll smash that fucking computer to bits one day, I swear it, to fucking bits. Get your fat fucking arse down here. I want to see a fucking wife in my house when I come through my front door. You hear me up there?

## Scene Two

*The kitchen.*

MICHAEL: So, you exist then.

MAEVE: Don't be angry, love. I was only...

MICHAEL: Angry?

MAEVE: I was only cleaning around.

MICHAEL: Angry?

MAEVE: You know you like things clean.

MICHAEL: You call this 'angry'?

MAEVE: And you'd be angrier if you saw dust on the stairs.

MICHAEL: You weren't on the fucking stairs, you were buried in your fucking hideaway.

MAEVE: Got to clean everywhere, haven't I?

MICHAEL: Regret the day I let you buy that contraption.

MAEVE: Best birthday present you could get me.

MICHAEL: Two fucking birthdays and two fucking Christmases in one, that little lot.

MAEVE: Wish you wouldn't swear so much.

MICHAEL: Should've bought you a fucking anchor instead, to keep you down here on fucking earth.

MAEVE: Please don't swear so much, love.

MICHAEL: Fuck, fuck, fuck. A fucking anchor chained round your fucking neck.

*MAEVE gives up, resigned. MICHAEL takes off his boots and puts on trainers.*

MAEVE: I've made you something special.

MICHAEL: Some foreign muck again?

MAEVE: You call it that but you know you enjoy it.

MICHAEL: You know me so well, don't you?

MAEVE: Well, we've had some years together.

MICHAEL: No longer a surprise to you, am I?

MAEVE: Oh, come on, love.

MICHAEL: Sooner have a box of chocolates than me, eh?

MAEVE: Why ever would I compare you to a box of chocolates?

MICHAEL: At least there's a surprise with every bite.

*MAEVE smiles.*

MICHAEL: Ha! Got you there! Topped my clever wife for a change.

MAEVE: You're always topping me, clever husband. And full of surprises you are.

MICHAEL: So what foreign muck is it this time?

MAEVE: I thought I'd try my hand at some Italian muck.

MICHAEL: Fucking Italian?

MAEVE: Nothing too exotic.

MICHAEL: Oh. 'Exotic.' Oh, oh! 'Nothing too exotic.' Oh dear, no. 'Nothing tooooooo exotic.' I fucking hope not. I hope fucking not.

MAEVE: Just a spaghetti Bolognaise.

MICHAEL: Oh, yes, well – I've heard of that one.

MAEVE: Don't be daft, Michael, you've done more than 'heard' of it, you've eaten it. Many times. In restaurants. You like sucking the spaghetti off the prongs. So I thought I'd please you and give you some of the foreign muck homemade.

MICHAEL: And where did we learn to cook it? You didn't waste my money on cook books, did you? Waste my money on fucking cook books, did you?

MAEVE: No, soft, went to the library, didn't I.

MICHAEL: Oh. Yes. The fucking library. Might've guessed that one. Spend all your time in the fucking library, don't you?

MAEVE: Please, Michael...

MICHAEL: Wake up one morning and find you gone. Maeve? Maeve? Where's my Maeve? Anyone seen my bookworm-wife? Yes, she's gone sleeping with the fucking books, hidden between sheets of old print, humping all those famous fucking writers.

MAEVE: It would be so much more pleasant to have a conversation without...

MICHAEL: You mean have a talk.

MAEVE: Without swearing every other word.

MICHAEL: Very prim, my wife.

MAEVE: I'm not prim.

MICHAEL: Got a delicate soul. There! 'Delicate.' I can use long words too, if I want. 'Delicate.' 'Delicate soul.' Long words and swear words.

MAEVE: I'll lay the table.

MICHAEL: I can use long words, but you can't swear.

MAEVE: I can swear.

MICHAEL: Show me.

MAEVE: I just don't choose to.

MICHAEL: Dare you.

MAEVE: Fuck, fuck, fuck. There! Nothing to it, but I'd prefer not to talk out of an impoverished vocabulary.

MICHAEL: A what?

MAEVE: An impoverished vocabulary.

*MICHAEL is dangerous.*

MICHAEL: That what you think I've got?

MAEVE: Oh, come on, Michael, let's eat.

MICHAEL: How many times must I tell you – no long words.

MAEVE: I'm sorry.

MICHAEL: No long fucking words in my house.

MAEVE: I said I'm sorry.

MICHAEL: I run a simple house. Nothing too fucking exotic in my house.

MAEVE: Let's eat.

MICHAEL: We're from simple stock.

MAEVE: Let's eat and talk of other things.

MICHAEL: Simple, honest stock.

MAEVE: (*Quoting*) Of ships and string and sealing-wax, and cabbages and kings.

*MAEVE's attempt to defuse the moment misfires.*

MICHAEL: And fucking poetry as well! Have you gone stark raving fucking mad?

MAEVE: I was only trying to amuse you.

MICHAEL: Amuse me? Amuse me? With fucking poetry?

MAEVE: The Italian muck will burn.

MICHAEL: Let it fucking burn. And when it's burnt, stick it up your fucking fat arse. I'm going down the road for fish and chips and a pint. (*He leaves.*)

## Scene Three

*MAEVE is in her attic hideaway. At her desktop, she composes and types.*

MAEVE: Shall I compare thee to a Cadbury's box?
   Thou art surprising with each bite I take.
   Thy many centres do my passions rouse
   While my own centre moistens sweetly for thy sake.

*She pauses to recount the last line.*

   While my own centre moistens sweetly for thy sake.

Twelve beats there, Maeve, should be ten – fourteen lines of ten beats each. Iambic pentameters. Pa-dum pa-dum pa-dum pa-dum pa-dum. Try again.

   Your many centres do my passions rouse... er...
   Your many centres do my passions rouse...

*She is struggling, until slowly shaping:*

   While my sweet centre moistens for thy sake...

No.

   While soft my centre moistens for thy sake.

172

Good. So:

> Shall I compare thee to a Cadbury's box?
> Thou art surprising with each bite I take
> Thy many centres do my passions rouse
> While soft my centre moistens for thy sake.

*Pause.*

Is he surprising with each bite? And does your soft centre moisten for his sake?

*Pause.*

Does your poor soft centre moisten? And why should it make him smile, anyway? He won't know the original. Can't say you married a man who shares your 'cultural framework' can you? And why not, Maeve, why didn't you marry such a man? (*She considers it.*) Because you didn't have a cultural framework when you married, did you, lovely? Didn't know your arse from your tit when he and thee were first acquent. All bonking, lager, and Punk Rock. (*She dances as she did aged seventeen.*) Except he wasn't even a punk. Too much colour. (*The banality of the movements amaze her.*) What did we think we were doing? Bit like a fast march gone wrong. One two three four, one two three four, left right, left right, left right, left right. (*She stops.*)

> Shall I compare thee to a summer's day?
> Thou art more lovely and more temperate...

*She savours the words.*

> More lovely and more temp-er-rate...

173

*She continues.*

> Rough winds do shake the darling buds of May,
> And summer's lease hath all too short a date.

*She considers this.*

You're thirty and seven months, Maeve, nearly half your summer's gone.

*Pause.*

The lease is all too short.

## Scene Four

*The kitchen. Late evening. An apprehensive MAEVE watches her husband drunkenly struggle to unlace and remove his trainers.*

MICHAEL: What you staring at?

MAEVE: Cat can look at the king.

MICHAEL: Your king, am I?

MAEVE: You might need help.

MICHAEL Kings don't need help.

MAEVE: Kings need entire kingdoms.

MICHAEL: Fucking reply for everything haven't you? Ever be a time when you won't have a reply? Never a thing I can say but you can't cap it. Not one day goes by I can say something and you'll say, 'That's right, Michael. I agree with you, Michael. Couldn't have said it better myself, Michael.' Not one fucking day. (*There is a cup near by. MICHAEL smashes it.*) That's better. Expressed myself just then, I did. You write fucking poetry an' I smash fucking cups an' things.

*MAEVE moves to pick up the pieces.*

MICHAEL: LEAVE IT!

MAEVE: You're walking around in socks.

MICHAEL: LEAVE IT!

MAEVE: You'll get bits in your feet – don't be daft.

*MICHAEL grabs her.*

MICHAEL: Don't call me daft.

*MICHAEL slaps a hand across her head.*

MICHAEL: Don't call me fucking daft. Never call me daft. What am I, something out of the loony bin? Not quite right, up there? Soft in the head? Never, never, never call me daft. Got my meaning?
    There! That's better. Expressed myself just then, I did. You write poetry, I smash cups an' things.

MAEV: If you didn't drink...

MICHAEL: Drink? Me? Me, drink? Not me. That's another person drinks, not me. When I drink a pint of beer I become another person who wants a pint of beer, drinks

175

that pint and becomes another person who wants a pint of beer, drinks that and...

MAEVE: Becomes another person who wants... ad infinitum...

*MICHAEL slaps a hand across her face.*

MICHAEL: No long words!

*MICHAEL beats her continuously. Their words merge, overlap, jumble.*

MICHAEL: You never listen! No long fucking words in my house. I keep telling you. You never learn 'cos you never listen...

MAEVE: Stop it, Michael, stop, for God's sake. It wasn't a long word, it was Latin for on and on and on and...

MICHAEL: Not even an English long word. Fucking Latin! How come you could be so clever?

MAEVE: I'm not...

MICHAEL: Fucking Latin!

MAEVE: I don't know any other Latin words.

MICHAEL: Christ almighty! Who did I fucking marry? You weren't like this when I married you. You knew nothing when I married you. When we stood in front of that registrar you barely knew your mouth from your cunt and now they're both dry as them rows and rows of useless

176

books there. Fucking Latin? Think you're cleverer than me do you? Cleverer? Cleverer? Fucking cleverer than me?

*MICHAEL gives MAEVE one final kick. He is spent. He weeps. He crawls to her, in remorse. He takes her in his arms.*

MICHAEL: Sorry. Sorry. Sorry. Sorry. Sorry. Sorry. Sorry. Sorry. Sorry.... (*He seems unable to stop.*)

*Long pause.*

MICHAEL: Maeve? Maeve? Will you gimme? Will you gimme? Will you gimme? You know, will you?

*MAEVE slowly, painfully, unbuttons her blouse, takes out a breast, cups it for him. MICHAEL slides down to suck. The beaten one comforts.*

MAEVE: Michael, will you let me look for a job? You've got yours. Very satisfying it must be – joinery. Making things fit. Wish I could make things fit. There's not much round here, I know, but something... bring in a few more bob, get me out of the house...

MICHAEL: (*Almost asleep*) Don't want neighbours to think I can't support my family.

MAEVE: We don't have a family, Michael.

MICHAEL: One day...

*Slow FADE.*

## Scene Five

*The kitchen. Morning. A sheepish husband eating cereal. A bruised wife making real coffee.*

MICHAEL: Snap, crackle and pop. Overgrown kid, aren't I?

*Pause.*

MICHAEL: Need to leave kiddie-times behind, right, Maeve?

MAEVE: Right, Michael.

*Silence.*

MICHAEL: Got an interesting job to start this morning.

MAEVE: Oh? What's that?

MICHAEL: The boss got asked by a bank to design a desk, and he designed this desk to sit on an upside-down cone, see? And he's worked everything out on paper – full size, gotta be full size, and he's cut out all his plywood shapes, and we're now gonna see if all his workings-out will work out.

MAEVE: That does sound interesting.

MICHAEL: It is, it is.

MAEVE: Making things that fit.

MICHAEL: Now he's a clever man, the boss. A clever man and a half, that one.

MAEVE: I'd like to work at a job where things fit.

MICHAEL: You write poems an' stuff.

MAEVE: Not very good poems an' stuff. (*She stumbles from a leftover pain.*)

MICHAEL: I'm sorry, love. Honest. I'm really, really sorry.

*MAEVE pours hot water through the filter.*

MICHAEL: Do you believe me, that I am?

MAEVE: I always believe you, that you are.

MICHAEL: Really, really sorry.

*Silence.*

MICHAEL: I've got to admit, that coffee sets me up for the day.

*MAEVE doesn't respond.*

MICHAEL: Well and truly sets me up.

*MAEVE doesn't respond.*

MICHAEL: Can't think now how I ever drank that Nescafé. Used to burn my stomach up. Bloody acid.

*MAEVE doesn't respond.*

MICHAEL: Good smell, too. You've changed my life round quite a bit you know – poetry and foreign muck.

*MAEVE doesn't respond.*

MICHAEL: Got something you can read me while I drink my dark mud?

*MAEVE doesn't respond.*

MICHAEL: 'Cos it is dark as mud you know, this coffee. Dark, dark as mud.

*MAEVE doesn't respond.*

MICHAEL: Notice I haven't sweared? No eff word all morning.

*MAEVE doesn't respond.*

MICHAEL: Coffee dark as mud.

*Long silence.*

MAEVE: Shall I compare thee to a Cadbury's box?
   Thou art surprising with each bite I take.
   Thy many centres do my passions rouse
   While soft my centre moistens for thy sake.

*Long pause.*

*MICHAEL drinks his coffee, suppresses his fury.*

MICHAEL: Inspired you, did I? Yes. Well. We'll talk about it later. When I'm back from work. You can explain it then. After we've eaten some foreign muck. Got some foreign muck planned for this evening, have we? Something not too exotic simmering away in that clever head of yours? Nothing too-oooooo exotic?

## Scene Six

*MAEVE's attic hideaway. Out of the darkness comes MAEVE's voice. The LIGHTS slowly build to find her, as before, trying to learn and deliver, this time from 'Hamlet'.*

MAEVE: (*Quoting*) Why, she would hang on him
       As if increase of appetite had grown
       By what it fed on; and yet, within a month –
       Let me not think on't! –
       Frailty, thy name is woman –
       A little month, or ere those shoes were old
       With which she followed my poor father's body
       Like Niobe, all tears – why, she –
       O God! A beast that wants discourse of reason
       Would have mourn'd longer –
       Married with my uncle,
       My father's brother, but no more like my father
       Than I to Hercules. Within a month,
       Ere yet the salt of most unrighteous tears
       Had left the flushing in her galled eyes,
       She married – O most wicked speed! To post
       With such dexterity to incestuous sheets!
       It is not, nor it cannot come to good.
       But break, my heart, for I must hold my tongue!

*Long pause.*

Oh, God, how I do love the language of the man.

It is not, nor it cannot come to good.

But break, my heart, for I must hold my tongue!

Must I? Are you aware, Maeve Lewis, what a privilege it is to be alive with him? Living in the world he lived in? Lives in? No matter that they're tragedies that he writes, they bring me joy. Isn't that strange, now? The death of Cordelia makes me weep and brings me joy. To know a man existed who could carve such shapes out of his life – that's so reassuring, so bloody reassuring in this bleak existence I've landed myself with. Trouble is, he brings on longings. That's what I really can't bear, he brings on longings to be somewhere else, to be someone else. And I can't fulfil them, these longings, this sense of – Oh, I don't know – other! I can't bloody well fulfil them.

But break, my heart, for I must hold my tongue.

Oh, God. The language, the language.

## Scene Seven

*MAEVE's attic hideaway. MICHAEL is present, and drunk.*

MICHAEL: Thought I'd pay a visit. Don't mind, do you, love?

*MAEVE shakes her head.*

MICHAEL: Your space – privacy an' all that – sure you don't mind?

MAEVE: Welcome.

182

MICHAEL: Welcome?

MAEVE: My world is your world.

MICHAEL: Oh? That's true, is it? Your world is my world?

MAEVE: That's how I've always wanted it to be.

MICHAEL: What, privacy an' all that?

MAEVE: I've got nothing private from you, Michael.

MICHAEL: Right, then. Let's talk about this, then. Let's sit and have what you call 'a conversation'. Not sure why 'a talk' isn't good enough, never mind – 'a conversation'. (*He slithers to the floor. Leans against her desk.*) 'My world is your world,' you say. I got it right? Those were your words, right? Am I right? Well fucking answer me, have I got it right? Oops! Mustn't swear. Tried. Promised myself on the way back – no fucking swearing. Oh, well, you'll have to put up with it. Not too much. Just now and again. Can't break habits over night. So, am I right? 'My world is your world,' you said.

MAEVE: That's what I said.

MICHAEL: Good. Now, here's a thing. Why can't it be the other way round? Why can't it be that my world is your world? Eh? Why can't it be that?

*Long wait.*

MICHAEL: 'Cos you hate my world, don't you? Say it, ''Cos I hate your world, Michael.'

183

MAEVE: What is your world, Michael?

MICHAEL: Well it's not fucking books with long words that's for sure.

*Silence. MAEVE is terrified of provoking him.*

MICHAEL: Lost your tongue? 'Conversation' come to an end? Finished? Michael not clever enough to have a conversation with?

*No response.*

*MICHAEL rises to his feet, moves to leave.*

MICHAEL: Oh well, fucking boring up here. Get more 'conversation' with my fucking telly than my fucking wife.

MAEVE: (*Trying*) Michael...

*MICHAEL is held.*

MICHAEL: Oh. Conversation?

MAEVE: How would you like to die?

MICHAEL: Why? Thinking of creeping up on me one night?

MAEVE: No, be serious.

MICHAEL: About dying?

MAEVE: You wanted to talk.

MICHAEL: (*Incredulous*) About fucking dying?

MAEVE: I was listening to 'Woman's Hour' on the radio, and the topic came up: how would you like to die? In your sleep? Suddenly, of a heart attack? Slowly, of old age, with time to say goodbye? How? How would you like to die?

MICHAEL: Unsuccessfully!

*MAEVE laughs with surprise and delight.*

MAEVE: Oh, Michael. I could kiss you to death when you're pleasant and witty. You're so sweet when you're witty.

MICHAEL: Sweet and witty, was I? Come as a surprise? (*He moves to her books, picks one out and looks at it.*) I can be ever so sweet if I like. (*He throws the book into her rubbish basket. Picks another.*) I can be ever so witty, too, if I like. (*Throws book. Picks another.*) Sweet an' witty. (*Throws book. Picks another.*) Anything I like. (*Throws book. Picks another. Reads.*) 'The Roob-i-yat of Oh-ma-ker-yam.' Fucking poetry! (*Throws book. Picks another. Reads.*) 'The Idiot' by Fido Dost... Dost... Dost... oi... fucking foreign muck. Don't tell me you actually read all this fucking foreign muck?

MAEVE: It's foreign but it's not mu...

MICHAEL: And you spend money on it?

MAEVE: Only secondhand, Michael, a few bob every now and then.

MICHAEL: (*Throws book. Picks another. Reads.*) 'Of Mice and Men' by John Steinbeck. Fucking German!

MAEVE: No, he's...

MICHAEL: A fucking Jew, then.

MAEVE: American. Won the Nobel Prize for Literature in 19-something-or-other. You'd like him.

MICHAEL: I would, would I?

MAEVE: He's simple, but...

MICHAEL: Oh, I'd like him 'cos he's fucking simple, would I?

MAEVE: You didn't let me finish. He's simple but profound.

MICHAEL: (*Bursting*) No fucking long words. (*He sweeps the books off the shelves.*)

MAEVE: No, Michael, no.

MICHAEL: How many times do you have to be told?

MAEVE: Oh, Christ, Michael, when will it all stop?

MICHAEL: This is my house, bought with my money, and I'll have what I want in it. No fucking long words.

*MICHAEL picks up something heavy to smash the screen of her desktop. MAEVE restrains him. The price is a beating.*

MICHAEL: You never learn. I try and I try and I try and I try but you do it on purpose. On purpose! Use words you know I won't understand so's to make me small. Well-I-won't-fucking-have-it. I-will-not-be-made-in-to-a-fucking-

186

moron.  Hear  me?  I-will-not-be-made-in-to-a-fucking-moron.

*Each word has been a punch. MICHAEL is spent. MAEVE moans with pain. As before, as always, remorse strikes him.*

MICHAEL: Sorry, sorry, sorry, sorry, sorry, sorry, sorry, sorry, sorry, sorry...

*And, as before, he holds her, weeps. And, as before, she cups her breast for him.*

*Slow FADE.*

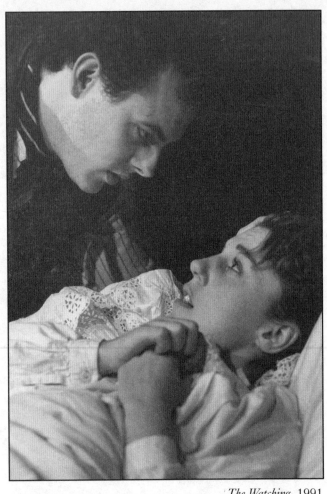

*The Watching*, 1991

# Playwrights and Companies

### Gwent Theatre
Established in 1976, Gwent Theatre provides a high quality professional theatre in education and youth theatre service for schools and communities. Productions, performances and workshops create access and participation for young people to experience live theatre and to develop an appreciation of literature and the performing arts.

### Hijinx Theatre
Hijinx was born in 1981. They began by devising new works, then regularly commissioned new works from other playwrights. Between 1990 and 2007, Hijinx commissioned twenty plays, some of which were for community audiences, while some were for adults with learning disabilities.

### Gillian Clark
Poet, playwright, editor, translator, and president of Ty Newydd writers' centre. Her poetry is studied by GCSE and A Level students throughout Britain and her work has been translated into ten languages, to date.

### Charles Way
Winner of the Writers Guild Best Chldren's Play Award and the Arts Council of England's Children's Award. Many of his plays have been performed worldwide and translated into other langauges. He has written for TV and radio, and his work has been broadcast by BBC Radio Four.

### Arnold Wesker
Prizewinning author of forty-two plays, four books of short stories, two collections of essays, a book for young people and three non-fiction titles. His works – including TV, radio and film scripts – continue to be performed worldwide.